WORLD WAR II
FOR BEGINNERS

WRITERS AND READERS PUBLISHING, INCORPORATED
P.O. Box 461, Village Station
New York, NY 10014

Text Copyright © 1991 Errol Selkirk
Illustrations © 1991 Naomi Rosenblatt and Shey Wolvek-Pfister
Cover Design: Chris Hyde

A Writers and Readers Documentary Comic Book
Copyright © 1991
ISBN # 0-86316-103-0
1 2 3 4 5 6 7 8 9 0

Manufactured in the United States of America

Beginners Documentary Comic Books are published by Writers and
Readers Publishing, Inc. Its trademark, consisting of the words
"For Beginners, Writers and Readers Documentary Comic Books"
and Writers and Readers logo, is registered in the U.S. Patent and
Trademark Office and in other countries.

WORLD WAR II
For Beginners

Written by Errol Selkirk

Illustrations & design by Naomi Rosenblatt and
Shey Wolvek-Pfister

> *To Donald Selkirk, who taught me
> there are some things worth fighting
> for. And to the memory of the six
> million and all the other innocent
> victims of this terrible war.*

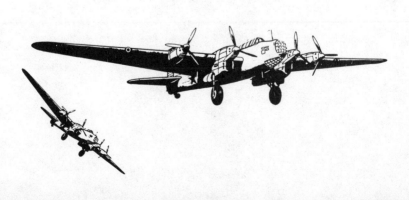

CONTENTS

INTRODUCTION

World War II was the greatest conflict in human history. It lasted nearly six years and cost the lives of over 40 million men, women, and children—at least half of them unarmed civilians.

All wars may be hell. But no struggle in modern times was more hellish than World War II. Between 1939 and 1945, scores of cities were vaporized or turned into rubble. Entire nations and peoples were exterminated. And terrible new weapons of destruction were introduced that continue to threaten the very existence of the human race.

World War II was **Total War**. For the first time in history, the absolute power of the modern industrial state was thrown into the fight. The fighting was not simply on distant battlefields. It was fought on the economic, social, and even psychological fronts.

Everyone was involved. Not just the young farmers, workers, and students who suddenly found themselves in uniform with a gun in their hand. But also the millions of men and women in the **Resistance**, who had no uniforms and often no guns. And the millions who toiled round the clock in the factories or endured the terror of modern warfare in their homes and underground, in crowded bomb shelters. And finally, the generation of those who were children, those who will always carry the memories of war with them.

Military history, obviously, can only tell one part of this story. To really understand World War II, we must listen to all the people who were there and remember. Not just the leaders and the generals. But also the little people, the men and women in the street who despise war and yet are forced to suffer through it and survive.

Without their voices, we today will never comprehend what happened, and why, and why it must never happen again.

Chapter I: The Twilight Peace

World War One ended on the llth hour of the llth day of the llth month of 1918. After four bloody years of fighting, it was finally all quiet on the Western Front. Yet the causes of war did not disappear with the coming of peace. Tragically, the last shot fired in the First World War was the first shot fired in the Second.

Who will dominate Europe?

That was the question in both wars. The traditional leaders were England and France. But they were being challenged by an ambitious new superpower: Germany.

German-speaking peoples had long inhabited dozens of small kingdoms, principalities, and free cities in Central and Eastern Europe. They saw themselves as Bavarians or Austrians or Prussians — not Germans. Their energy and hard work produced great wealth and cultural achievements. But not political power.

A mighty German Empire was the dream of Count Otto von Bismarck, the advisor to King Wilhelm I of Prussia. Bismarck was brilliant, far-sighted, and ruthless. He believed the key to achieving Germany's rightful *place in the sun* was Prussian military might and rapid industrialization:

"Blood and Iron."

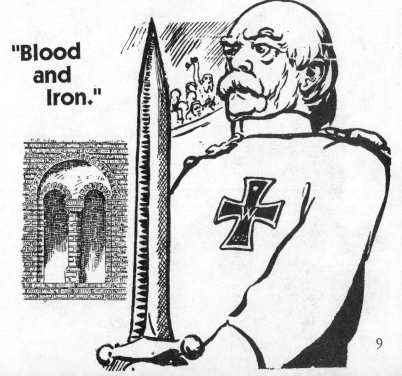

Prussia began by swallowing up its smaller German neighbors. In 1871, Bismarck was ready to challenge France, the strongest land power in Europe. After a series of quick, decisive battles, the Prussians defeated and humiliated the French.

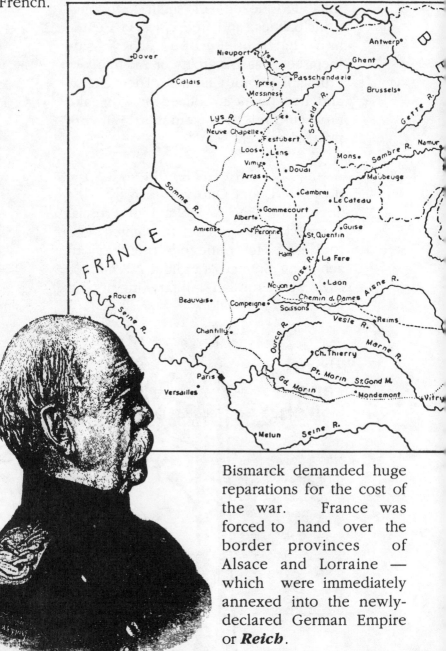

Bismarck demanded huge reparations for the cost of the war. France was forced to hand over the border provinces of Alsace and Lorraine — which were immediately annexed into the newly-declared German Empire or *Reich*.

When World War began in 1914, Germany was even stronger. It outnumbered France 3:2. And its industrial might was fast approaching that of Great Britain.

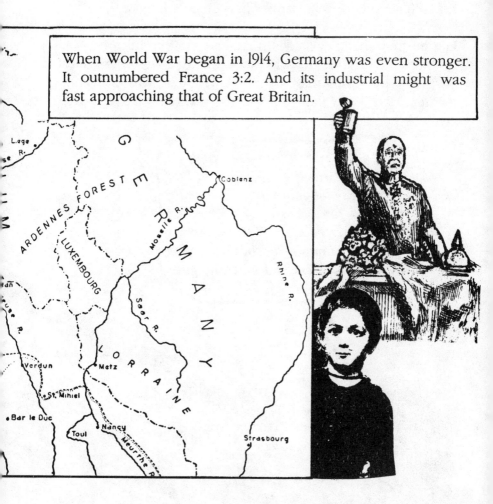

Yet the Reich was vulnerable. It was bound by Treaty to the crumbling and unpopular Austrian and Turkish Empires. And it was also forced to fight a two front war against 100 million Russians to the East, who had a treaty with the Anglo-French Allies.

On August 1, the fighting began with gallant calavary charges and daring bayonet attacks. – which were quickly crushed by massed machine guns, poison gas, and heavy cannon fire. Millions died. Both armies dug in for a long war.

Life in the trenches was death in slow motion. In three years of battle, neither side was able to advance beyond the barbed wire more than 10 miles. Here is how a combat soldier tried to explain the bizarre realities of that war to civilians :

> *"Dig a trench shoulder high in your garden, fill it half full of water and get in it. Remain there for two or three days on an empty stomach. Furthermore, hire a lunatic to shoot at you with revolvers and machine guns at close range."*

Imagine this savage existence lasting months, even years. The war became a bitter struggle of endurance. By 1917, the balance of power clearly began to tip against the German Emperor, **Kaiser** Wilhelm II.

Italy and the mighty USA had joined the fight against Germany.

At sea, a powerful British Naval blockade tightened the economic noose around the Reich.

On land, the German Army still occupied large sections of France, Belgium, and Russia. But it was desperately short of food, ammunition, and replacements for the front. Army doctors were now drafting the young, the old, practically anyone who could walk on two legs.

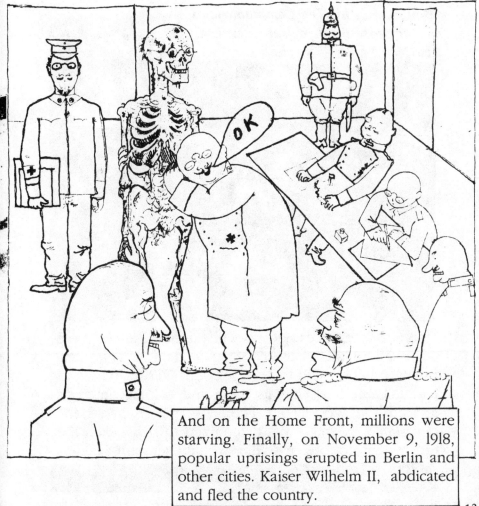

And on the Home Front, millions were starving. Finally, on November 9, 1918, popular uprisings erupted in Berlin and other cities. Kaiser Wilhelm II, abdicated and fled the country.

A new government was formed by civilians unprepared for the harsh realities of power. Led by moderate Social Democrats, Germany now hoped to end the war on the generous terms set down by U.S. President **Woodrow Wilson**.

Wilson tried to impose American ideals of peace and freedom on a planet which had never known anything but war. He proposed a **14 Point Program** calling for free elections, free trade, freedom of the seas, and world disarmament. And he spoke of creating a mighty League of Nations to guarantee the peace.

"God gave us his Ten Commandments, and we broke them. Wilson gave us his Fourteen Points – we shall see."

Georges Clemenceau, the tough French Premier, was chairman of the peace conference held at Versailles. Britain was prepared to go along with Wilson so long as it didn't interfere with its trade and colonial interests around the world. But France – which had been devastated by war – was determined to so weaken the enemy that no foreign soldier would ever dare again to set foot in France.

It was decided that the Austrian Empire would be broken up to create independent Hungary, Czechoslovakia, and Yugoslavia. Germany would lose all its overseas colonies in Africa and Asia, as well as the provinces of Alsace and Lorraine. And a new nation, Poland, would be created at the expense of Prussia.

The German Reich would be demilitarized. Crushing war reparations were to be paid, equal to the cost of all the destruction in France. And there was a final humiliation: Berlin would have to accept sole guilt for causing the war.

When the new German government balked, the Allies threatened invasion. In the end, Berlin was forced to bow to the harsh Versailles *Diktat.* With the Treaty signed, the Allies turned away from the "German Problem" to their own pressing concerns.

But Germany's problems would not go away. Millions of veterans limped home to a shattered society. The economy was in ruins. People feared for the future. The Kaiser was gone, and with him went the old traditional value of obedience to authority.

REVOLUTION was in the air.

The Bolshevik Revolution in Russia, under the leadership of Vladimir Ilych **Lenin**, had toppled the government and seized control. Hungary burst into revolt. Paralyzing strikes erupted throughout Italy.

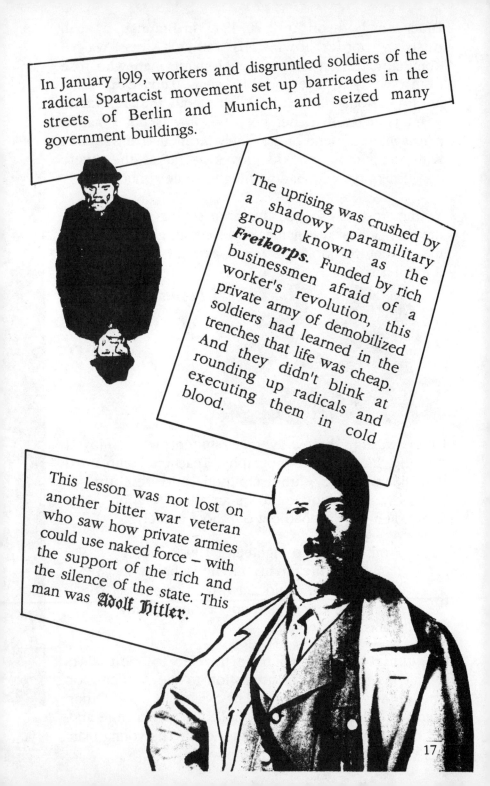

In January 1919, workers and disgruntled soldiers of the radical Spartacist movement set up barricades in the streets of Berlin and Munich, and seized many government buildings.

The uprising was crushed by a shadowy paramilitary group known as the **Freikorps.** Funded by rich businessmen afraid of a worker's revolution, this private army of demobilized soldiers had learned in the trenches that life was cheap. And they didn't blink at rounding up radicals and executing them in cold blood.

This lesson was not lost on another bitter war veteran who saw how private armies could use naked force — with the support of the rich and the silence of the state. This man was Adolf Hitler.

Hitler was born on April 20, 1889, in Braunau, a small Austrian border town. His father, Alois, was a dominating, short-tempered, self-made man who rose from poverty to a respectable civil service position as a customs inspector. Adolf's mother, Klara, was 23 years younger than her husband. It was not a happy marriage, as a friend of the family recalled: "He was strict with the family, no kid gloves as far as they were concerned; his wife had nothing to smile about."

Young Adolph escaped this grim setting by creating a dream world of war games and German glory, based on the adventure books he loved. Several local boys fell under his spell.

"I became the leader of a small gang."

Hitler was a below-average student who enjoyed drawing, history, and geography. Teachers complained that he was lazy, undisciplined, and resentful of authority. Yet he longed to be an artist. As soon as his father died, he dropped out of school entirely.

 From sixteen to eighteen, Hitler lived a pampered life at his mother's home in Linz. Here he could draw, read in peace, attend the Opera, and go for long dreamy walks in the country.

Everything changed when he traveled to **Vienna** to submit his drawings for admission to the Academy of Fine of Arts. To his shock, he was rejected. Other rejections followed when he applied to architecture and technical school. Then his mother died. The young man was shattered, totally adrift in the world.

From 1908 to 1913, Hitler lived a shifting, bohemian life in Vienna, the capital of the Austrian Empire. Here he slept in shabby furnished rooms and did the occasional odd job painting houses or portraits. Though his clothes were worn, his manners were always stiff and correct.

Only his intense seriousness distinguished him from thousands of other failures on the fringe of society. And his eyes. Many years later, childhood friend August Kubizek could still recall the impact Hitler's eyes made on people:

"Never in my life have I seen any other person whose appearance—how shall I put it —was so completely dominated by the eyes. It was uncanny how those eyes could change their expression, especially when he was speaking."

And he was always speaking. Hitler was drunk with words. Sometimes he spoke about the glories of art, of architecture, of music. Other times the conversation took a darker turn. For it was here that Adolf Hitler learned to make an art of hatred.

The rich, the educated, the aristocrats who had rejected him and his dreams of glory – they would be humbled.

The grubby workers he was forced to rub elbows with in Vienna's teeming soup kitchens and flophouses – they would be disciplined.

But a special fate was reserved for the foreigners who made him feel like an alien in his own country. Nothing in Hitler's smalltown background had prepared him for Vienna's ethnic diversity:

"I was repelled by the conglomeration of races which the capital showed me, repelled by this whole mixture of Czechs, Poles, Hungarians, Ruthenians, Serbs, and Croats, and everywhere, the eternal mushroom of humanity – Jews and more Jews."

Here he saw his first Eastern European Jews, dressed in traditional black caftan and hair locks. They repelled, frightened, and yet obsessed him. He soon began to read the crude anti-Semitic literature that flourished in Vienna. The Jews, he learned, were responsible for everything wrong with the world.

21

The outbreak of World War I rescued him from his rootless wandering. He immediately joined the mighty German Army, thriving on the easy camaraderie and discipline. Four years he fought in the trenches of the Western Front, serving with distinction as a courier. In 1918, he was awarded the Iron Cross First Class for valor — a rare decoration for someone rising no higher in the ranks than corporal.

When the Kaiser was overthrown Hitler went into a deep depression. It was now that he discovered his true vocation. His intense nationalism led his officers to appoint him political instructor to the troops. His superiors quickly realized his unusual gifts:

"Herr Hitler... is the born popular speaker, and by his fanaticism and his crowd appeal he clearly attracts the attention of the audience, and compels it to share his trend of thought."

In Munich, Hitler was sent by the Army to spy on a tiny nationalist group with a suspiciously socialist name -- The German Workers' Party. At his very first meeting, Hitler couldn't resist speaking out. The small gathering fell silent. After all the uncertainty of the modern era, here at last was someone to believe in again totally. Within a few months, Hitler had become their *Fuebrer,* or leader:

"It was feeling that led us to Hitler... He who once looked into Hitler's eyes, he who once heard him, will never get away from him again."

Within two years, Hitler had given the group a new identity and a new name: The National Socialist German Workers Party or **Nazis** for short. The party now had a flag which was red, black, and white. It had an insignia, the Swastika, the crooked cross which in ancient myth symbolized the sun and resurgence. And Hitler had given them a new slogan,

𝕲𝖊𝖗𝖒𝖆𝖓𝖞 𝕬𝖜𝖆𝖐𝖊

A paramilitary guard was formed — the **Sturmabteilung** — Stormtroopers. These Brownshirt bully boys policed Nazi meetings and terrorized enemies. But it was always the Fuehrer at the center of things.

The time had come for bold action. The economy was in shambles. German money was now worth less than the paper it was printed on. Millions of marks were needed to even buy a loaf of bread. By now, Hitler had learned from Italian Fascist leader, **Benito Mussolini,** how to be all things to all people:

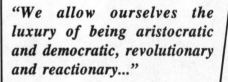

"We allow ourselves the luxury of being aristocratic and democratic, revolutionary and reactionary..."

In 1922, **Il Duce** had led his Fascist Black Shirts on a triumphant march on Rome. The Italian government hoped the **Fascisti** thugs would whip striking workers in line. Mussolini was given wide emergency powers. And within months, Italy was a dictatorship.

On November 8, 1923, Hitler gathered his followers in a beer hall in Munich and fired a pistol in the air. This was the signal for a **Putsch,** an uprising that was supposed to rally all Germany.

"No one can leave this hall. The National Revolution has begun. The Army is with us!"

The revolt failed when local policemen fired on the Nazis, killing 16, and driving the rest into hiding. Hitler was arrested and put on trial for high treason. He skillfully used the proceedings as a political forum. Soon all Germany knew of him.

25

Sentenced to five years in comfortable confinement in Landsburg Prison, Hitler used his time well. He strolled the picturesque grounds, entertained visitors, and even dictated a book. This rambling work was called **Mein Kampf** -- My Struggle. Its view of the world was often crude, illogical, and based on false premises. Yet Hitler's prophetic tone and his call for German supremacy touched millions who also found themselves lost in the modern world.

There were just three simple rules to follow.

The first was **Struggle**:

> *"Those who want to live, let them fight, and those who do not want to fight in this world of eternal struggle do not deserve to live."*

And the last was **Leadership.** Strong leaders would give the Master Race the discipline it needed to seize power.

> *"The movement advocates the principle of the unconditional authority of the leader, coupled with the greatest responsibility...Only a hero is called for..."*

Next was **Race**. From the crackpot anti-Semitism he had absorbed in Vienna, Hitler came to believe that there was such a thing as the Aryan Race. These were the tall, blond, blue-eyed northern Europeans who were biologically destined to rule the world:

> *"All human culture, all the results of art, science, and technology that we see before us today, are almost exclusively the creative product of the Aryan."*

Hitler was that man. He would be strong and ruthless in the eternal struggle against Germany's worst enemy: the **Jew.**

For Hitler, even the crudest anti-Semitic stereotypes were true: Jews are all the same. They are a Race, the mirror image of the noble Aryan. They are a virus, a plague on the planet with no culture of their own. All they do is destroy and contaminate:

"Your Jew is and remains the typical parasite, a sponger who like a noxious bacillus keeps spreading... Wherever he appears, the host people dies out."

Hitler now began to attract supporters from the upper classes. After only nine months in prison, powerful friends got him released. He was still young enough to learn from failure. The German people, he now realized, were too orderly to support a direct assault on the government.

Instead, Hitler would turn the weakness of democracy against itself. Backed by the iron fist of his Stormtroopers, he would skillfully exploit free speech, free press, and free elections to put an end to freedom. Then the real Nazi revolution would finally begin.

27

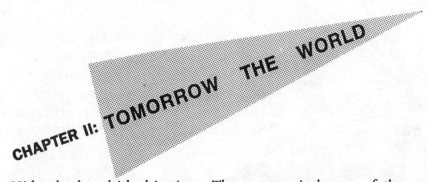

CHAPTER II: TOMORROW THE WORLD

Hitler had to bide his time. The economic boom of the **Roaring Twenties** finally caught up with Germany. People were happy to let the Republic manage things.

The government moved its capital away from Berlin in militaristic Prussia to **Weimar**, a small town known for art and philosophy. Everywhere there was a rebirth of cultural life.

At the national art institute called the **Bauhaus,** young designers and architects were radically changing the way the world looked. And in the theatre, Bertholt Brecht was changing the way people looked at the world, linking art and politics in a new way.

The visionary films of Fritz Lang — like the paintings of Expressionists Georg Grosz, Otto Dix, and Max Beckmann — tried to strip off the shiny surface of modern life to expose its nightmare side. German artists like these seemed to sense that civilization could disappear at any moment into a dark night of savagery.

Others tried to dance the night away, fueled by alcohol, cocaine, and

Hot American Jazz

Berlin became the capital of sex. Nudity was as common as champagne in the city's teeming cabarets. Yet there was something unreal, even desperate to all the merrymaking.

Reality intruded on **Black Tuesday**, October 29, 1929—
the day of the great New York Stock Market crash.
International business collapsed suddenly. Within months,
thousands of German companies went bankrupt. Factories
cut production and fired millions of workers.

So began the **Great Depression**. By 1932, a third of all
German workers was out of a job and on a breadline.
This disaster was bound to have major social
consequences in Germany.

"When we Germans cannot work, we go crazy."

The shaky Weimar Republic was powerless. Germans,
inexperienced with democracy, were growing impatient.
Nazis battled Communists in the streets with guns and
clubs. Extremists gained strength in the elections of 1930 —
at the expense of the moderates.

Overnight, the Nazis went from the smallest party in the
Reichstag, the German parliament, to the second largest.
Only the badly-weakened Social Democrats were still
stronger.

New elections were scheduled for July 1932. Hitler now needed money and support from the rich, who feared this odd Austrian upstart and his crude Brownshirt army. **Herman Goering** stepped in to help. Goering was a well-born World War I fighter ace. When the Versailles Treaty abolished the Air Force, Goering lost his job. But he found a cause:

We love Adolf Hitler because we believe, with a faith that is deep and unshakeable, that he was sent to us by God to save Germany.

Hitler appeared before an elite group of industrialists attired in a dark business suit. He spoke for two and a half hours without once mentioning the word "Jew." Only the Nazis, he declared, were capable of keeping the workers in their place.

Yet a few days later, he turned around and told a group of workers that he was truly a man of the people:

To me everyone is entirely equal. What interest do the intellectuals have for me, the middle class, or the proletariat? I am interested only in the German people.

Hitler was a genius at manipulating the individual's need to believe in something greater than himself. He was ably assisted by his propaganda wizard, **Josef Goebbels.**

Dr. Goebbels was intelligent, eloquent, and ruthless. He began life as a poor child, crippled in one leg. A charity put him through school, where he eventually obtained a doctorate. After years of effort, Goebbels remained a miserable failure as a writer. Now he was given the job of shaping the Fuehrer's public image. Soon he would change the whole face of German culture.

The German elections of 1932 gave the Nazis an impressive 38% of vote. A temporary alliance with conservative business parties lent the Nazis a working majority in the Reichstag. The industrialists foolishly assumed they could use the little Bavarian Corporal to serve their own ends. In January 1933, they agreed to make him Chancellor. They thought:

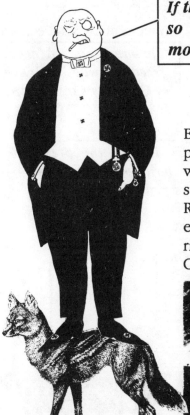

If the jackel is not so hungry, he is more easily tamed.

Ecstatic Nazis staged torchlight parades all over Germany. A few weeks after this triumph, a suspicious fire destroyed the Reichstag building. Hitler used the emergency to suspend human rights guaranteed by the Weimar Constitution.

Now, any individual, any group, could be imprisoned without a trial. Hitler got the Reichstag to give him the power to create laws at will. Finally, on July 14, 1933, the Nazi Party became the only political party in Germany.

Hitler moved quickly to consolidate power. The governing principle of the new regime was *Gleichschaltung* or alignment. Everyone would have to get in step:

> *"We have to put a stop to the idea that it's part of everybody's civil rights to say whatever he pleases."*

lawyers were whipped into line.

> *"The action of the Fuehrer was pure justice. It is not subject to the law; instead it was the highest law."*

So were many intellectuals:

> *"The much praised 'academic freedom' will be driven out of Germany's institutions."*

And newspapers:

> *"What is necessary is that the press blindly follow the basic principle — the leadership is always right."*

And the churches:

> *"One nation! One God! One Reich! One church!"*

Racial enemies like the Jews were purged from universities, hospitals, newspapers, the film industry, and many other occupations. Jewish shops were boycotted. Soon Jews would lose all rights.

Political enemies were methodically crushed. The purge began with Communists, then turned to Socialists, labor leaders, moderate Social Democrats, and anyone still foolish enough to believe in democracy. Next came those brave Catholics, Protestants, and Jehovah Witnesses who resisted religious alignment.

Prisoners were interrogated by the **Gestapo,** the dreaded Secret Police. Then they were sent to concentration camps to be systematically dehumanized by brutality, work, and hunger. The first such miniature barbed wire hell was **Dachau.**

Hitler now turned on the rough, unruly Stormtroopers who had put him into power. Brownshirt leaders were loudly demanding more weapons and more power in the new regime. The Fuehrer decided that they too would have to be aligned in a bloody purge.

He turned to his own elite body guard—the highly disciplined men of the **SCHUTZSTAFFEL** or **S.S.** These agents of death wore well-tailored black uniforms marked with Death's Head insignias and double lightning bolts. And their ruthless commander was a failed chicken farmer named **Heinrich Himmler**.

In August 1934, Hitler officially assumed the title of Fuehrer of the Third German Reich. Over 80% of all German voters approved this step in a special vote. With the nation firmly behind him, he could turn his gaze to bigger things.

Today Germany - Tomorrow the World

Hitler's foreign policy was simple. Germany would become the dominant power in the world. The key to Nazi policy was the word **Lebensraum.** For Germans to achieve their rightful place in the sun, they would need "living room," additional lands for a growing population. Yet how does one acquire the lands of a neighbor? Not by peaceful trade. But by naked military might.

Now began the biggest secret rearmament in history. Civilian factories built bombers, tanks, and warships. Strategic highways were constructed throughout Germany. Unemployment disappeared as workers were sucked into the uniformed labor corps.

Even children were mobilized. The 𝔥𝔦𝔱𝔩𝔢𝔯 𝔶𝔬𝔲𝔱𝔥 movement combined hiking and camping with military drill. Each youth wore a brown uniform complete with a dagger that bore the motto Blood and Honor. Total obedience was the rule.

"What pulses through us is the pure faith you gave us. You and none else, my Fuehrer, are the way and the end."

Yet while he armed for war, Hitler spoke to the world of peace. A just peace. A peace in which Germany joined other nations as an equal, with the power to defend itself.

In late 1936, Hitler took his next big gamble. He sent a small military force into the Rhineland, a rich industrial area bordering France. This was a clear violation of the Versailles Treaty. But the French government was too divided, too worried about its own economic problems, to take strong action.

Mild protest came from London. Britain was still too deep in the Depression to worry about events far away on the continent. Besides, many influential people in the upper classes actually admired Hitler. He had crushed the Communists, after all, put Germany back to work, created order. Nazi militarism could certainly be **appeased** – once the Reich attained its rightful place in the sun.

In Germany itself, gigantic rallies were staged to unite the people in the cult of the Fuehrer. In Nuremburg, a hundred thousand gathered at night to the thunder of drums and trumpets. The individual was quickly submerged in a sea of stiff, uniformed bodies, chanting slogans.

"As Adolf Hitler is entering the Zeppelin Field, 150 floodlights of the Air Force blaze up... Nothing like it has ever been seen before. The wide field resembles a powerful Gothic Cathedral made of light."

"You cannot imagine how silent it becomes as soon as this man speaks; it is as if all are no longer able to breathe."

"I do not know how to describe the emotions that swept over me as I heard this man... I felt ready to spring on any enemy."

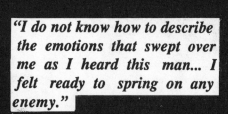

Germany was on the march. And it was not alone. The Great Depression had made the democracies unsure of themselves. Into this vacuum of power now stepped the dictators. Newsreels around the world capture the unending tide of aggression:

1935, 1936, 1937

Ethiopia. Mussolini's army invades this distant African kingdom. Modern weapons and even poison gas are used against barefoot tribesmen. Economic sanctions by League of Nations members fail to stop the Fascists — and the measures are soon lifted.

China. Japanese militarists launch an undeclared war of conquest. Terror bombing of civilians and widespread atrocities shock the world. Yet nothing is done.

Spain. General Francisco Franco leads an Army uprising against the democratic government in Madrid. To support Franco, Mussolini sends an army complete with tanks and artillery. Hitler orders the bombers of his Condor Legion to smash undefended Guernica. Thousands are murdered. Yet Washington, London, and Paris remain neutral.

Germany By 1938, the Reich devotes a fifth of its industrial output to preparation for war. On March 12, German troops cross the Austrian border in another violation of the Versailles Treaty. Hitler is met in Vienna by cheering thousands who welcome annexation.

London and **Paris** protest yet again. And yet again, nothing is done. British policy, in the words of a disgusted Anthony Eden of the Foreign Office, had become:

"Peace at almost any price."

Hitler now complains that German-speaking Czechs are oppressed by the government in Prague, the last democracy in Central Europe. The Fuehrer demands the annexation of the *Sudetenland,* the German-speaking, heavily-fortified mountainous area of western Czechoslovakia. And he will have it, even if it means war. The brave Czechs mobilize, fearing the worst.

Enter **Neville Chamberlain.** The British Prime Minister was a passionate believer in the power of reasonable men to reason together. Meeting Hitler in Munich, Chamberlain agreed to hand over the Sudetenland in return for the Fuehrer's lasting promise of peace.

"It is the last territorial demand I have to make in Europe. This is a guarantee."

On September 30, Chamberlain returned to England a hero. He had Herr Hitler's signature on the Munich document. This, he believed, guaranteed :

> ## *"Peace in our time."*

> We, the German Führer and Chancellor and the British Prime Minister, have had a further meeting today and are agreed in recognising that the question of Anglo-German relations is of the first importance for the two countries and for Europe.
>
> We regard the agreement signed last night and the Anglo-German Naval Agreement as symbolic of the desire of our two peoples never to go to war with one another again.
>
> We are resolved that the method of consultation shall be the method adopted to deal with any other questions that may concern our two countries, and we are determined to continue our efforts to remove possible sources of difference and thus to contribute to assure the peace of Europe.

"We have sustained a total and unmitigated defeat."

Winston Churchill had often denounced Hitler, but few listened. Though a member of Chamberlain's ruling Conservative Party, Churchill had been kept out of power for a decade. He was too stubborn, too independent. Now he warned that Czechoslovakia was helpless without the strong defenses of the Sudetenland. Events soon proved him right.

On March 15, 1939, German soldiers goose-stepped into stunned and embittered Prague.

This was the end of **appeasement**. Chamberlain had been tricked and humiliated, but his eyes were finally open.

On March 29, Britain offered Poland support against any Nazi attack. France soon followed. The British Parliament voted to double the military budget and introduced universal conscription. The Army began to mobilize. Yet these actions were too little and far too late.

The only power which could guarantee Polish independence was an old foe, the Soviet Union. Communist **Josef Stalin** was just as ruthless as Hitler, rising to ultimate power through intrigue and violence. He cleverly pitted the old Russian revolutionary leaders against each other. Then he had them murdered or shipped off to prison camps in Siberia -- along with millions of other luckless Soviets.

Yet it was in Stalin's own interest to stop Hitler. The U.S.S.R. had offered Britain and France an anti-Nazi pact to defend the Czechs before the sell-out in Munich. Chamberlain had refused. The British conservatives hated the Communists too much to even consider it. Now Stalin feared that the democracies were trying to push Hitler east. Quietly, Russia began to make its own plans for dealing with Germany.

The Nazis now began beating war drums about Poland's oppression of German-speaking people in the port city of Danzig. The Poles replied by mobilizing their large, though obsolete, army. Hitler's mind was made up. This time there would be war. He doubted that the English and French would really get involved. "Our opponents are little worms," he declared. "I saw them at Munich."

Hitler had one more ace up his sleeve. On August 23, l939, Germany and Russia signed a **Nonaggression Pact** which secretly divided Poland and eastern Europe. And while the world held its breath, the Fuehrer told his generals not to worry:

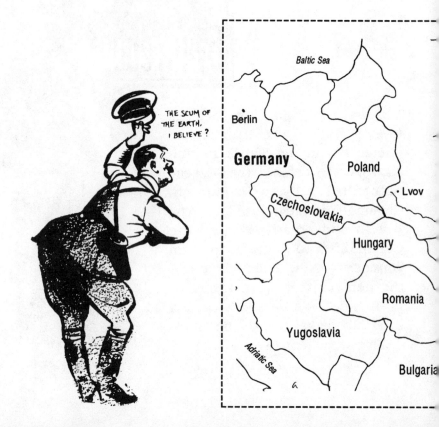

"I shall strike like lightning with the full force of a mechanized army of which Poland has no conception."

Yet the generals *were* worried. So Hitler reassured them. Once Poland was brought to its knees, Germany would convene a peace conference somewhere and settle matters. Chamberlain would be only too happy to agree. And the French would have to go along.

THE BLOODY ASSASSIN OF THE WORKERS, I PRESUME?

USSR

Kiev

Ukraine

Black Sea

This was the biggest miscalculation of Hitler's life. But it would not be the last.

CHAPTER III: THE STORM

On the morning of September 1, Poland awoke to the sound of **Blitzkrieg** — Hitler's Lightning War. Without warning, German *Stuka* dive bombers outfitted with sirens came screaming out of the clouds to spread terror and destruction.

Hermann Goering's *Luftwaffe* ruled the skies. In the first hours of the war, most of the tiny Polish Air Force was destroyed on the ground. Precision bombing then shattered Poland's ground defenses and scattered the shocked, demoralized soldiers.

Next came swift columns of *Panzer* tanks, smashing through enemy lines and plunging deep into the heart of the country, disrupting communications and spreading panic. Speed and shock was used to paralyze the Poles.

Tanks swept around strong resistance and encircled it. Infantry then moved in to mop up and take prisoners. Meanwhile, the Germans kept rolling toward Warsaw.

It was an unequal battle between man and machine, the past and the present. The Polish armies were cut off and quickly surrounded. In desperation, a brigade of Poland's famous calvary charged straight into the Panzers. Within minutes, the battlefield was littered with corpses of slaughtered horses and their riders.

On September 10, a large Polish force under command of General Bortnowski was trapped with its back to the River Bzura. Bortnowski ordered his men to break out of the tightening German noose, cross the river, and fall back toward Warsaw.

The Luftftwaffe suddenly struck from above, blasting bridges across the river and blocking all retreat. After nine days of bloody struggle, Bortnowski and 170,000 troops were finally forced to surrender.

The Poles now received another blow. As part of the deal Stalin signed with Germany, the Soviet Red Army crossed the border and occupied the eastern half of Poland. More than 200,000 Polish troops were rounded up and deported to Siberia. Thousands of officers were secretly massacred in the Katyn Forest. With this brutal stab in the back, Poland's chances of resistance disappeared.

Yet **Warsaw** remained defiant. In the Polish capital, civilians rushed to dig trenches and anti-tank barriers. German guns shelled the city relentlessly. Goering sent in the Luftwaffe. Two weeks of constant bombing reduced most of the city to rubble:

"Everywhere corpses, wounded humans, killed horses."

ANGLIO! TWOJE DZI

In flame and smoke, Warsaw was dying. On September 28, the government faced the inevitable and surrendered. Yet more than 100,000 Polish soldiers managed to escape through Rumania to the West. Here they carried on the fight.

On September 3, Britain and France honored their treaty obligations and declared war on Germany. Chamberlain was still in shock:

"Everything I have worked for, everything that I have hoped for, everything that I have believed in my public life, has crashed into ruins."

The Western Allies never believed they'd really have to fight. The English Army was still pitifully small. The French Army was much larger, but immobile. France trusted in the strength of the *Maginot Line*, a wall of fortresses hundreds of miles long that took nearly a decade and many billions of francs to construct.

Events would soon prove that Allied strategy was tragically flawed. It was based on the experience of the First War, and assumed that a tough defender could stop any attack. But the Blitzkrieg showed that speed, shock, and mobility could penetrate or bypass any static defence.

England and France decided to wait for Hitler to make the first move. They assumed the Maginot Line would force the Germans to attack by way of neutral Belgium in the north. The armies would once again fight it out in the trenches – just like the first war. And once again, British seapower would eventually starve Germany into total submission.

So began the *Sitzkrieg* – the Sitting War. Along the well-equipped Maginot Line, soldiers prepared for a long boring vigil:

"We're not fighting the enemy. We're fighting *l'ennui*."

The Fuehrer still hoped the Allies would make peace. He even demobilized part of the Wehrmacht, the mighty German Army. Not until late autumn did Hitler admit to himself that the only way to peace was to withdraw from Poland. This he would not do. Instead, he ordered plans for attacking the West. The result was one of the most brilliant military campaigns in history.

In December, Stalin took advantage of his pact with Hitler to attack neighboring **Finland.** The Finns were massively outnumbered, but they used guerilla tactics to stop the Soviets.

"For four miles the road and forests were strewn with the bodies of men and horses. The corpses were frozen as hard as petrified wood."

Stalin's paranoia made him suspect the loyalty of the Red Army. In 1938, he brutally purged most of his top generals. Now he was paying the price in shame. Yet the weight of Russian numbers eventually forced a truce on Moscow's terms. Hitler's eyes now also turned to the north.

In London, energetic Winston Churchill had been put in charge of the British Navy. The Fuehrer suspected that Churchill would use neutral Norway as a base to bottle up the German fleet in the North Sea.

Vidkun Quisling

A small flotilla of German warships carrying commandoes secretly sailed into Norwegian waters. On April 9, Hitler ordered paratroopers to seize Oslo's airport. Key cities and ports quickly fell to the invaders. A puppet government was soon formed under the leadership of pro-Nazi Vidkun Quisling. At the same time, Panzers rolled into neighboring, defenseless Denmark.

In response, Churchill landed an amphibious force at Narvik, a small port in northern Norway. Fierce fighting went on for a month. Then suddenly, London ordered the troops back from this distant battlefield. An utter catastrophe had occurred much closer to home.

The Battle in the West began exactly as the Allies expected — with a German invasion north of the Maginot Line. But the speed of the attack was a surprise.

On May 10, German paratroopers landed in Belgium, seizing key roads and bridges. Glider forces landed on top of powerful Belgian fortresses guarding the frontier, and destroyed them from above with high explosives. Panzers poured through the gap.

Holland was invaded the same day. The Germans brushed aside Dutch troops and drove to the sea. The Luftwaffe launched a fierce terror bombing of Rotterdam, which leveled the center of the city and killed thousands of civilians. On May 14, The Netherlands capitulated.

In London, the crisis forced Chamberlain to step aside. Winston Churchill now became Prime Minister. He told the British that they would have to struggle long and hard for victory. But without victory there could be no survival. To this cause, Churchill swore total dedication:

"I have nothing to offer but blood, toil, tears and sweat."

According to plan, Allied forces rushed north to meet the enemy. No one suspected that Hitler had set an ingenious trap. Soon the best soldiers in England and France, as well as most of their tanks and artillery, were parked side to side in a congested, muddy corner of Belgium.

That's when the real Blitzkrieg began – in France. Under cover of night, Panzers rolled through the dense, undeveloped Ardennes Forest, the one gap in the Maginot Line. Because the forest was considered impassable, the whole area was thinly defended.

When the Allies finally woke up to the danger, the Germans had already crossed the River Sedan. British air attacks on the bridges failed to slow the advance. Soon 1,800 Panzers were speeding towards Paris. Erwin **Rommel,** a German tank commander who would soon become a legend, described the Allied panic that followed:

> *"Always the same picture, troops and civilians in wild flight down both sides of the road... a chaos of guns, artillery, military vehicles of all kinds, inextricably entangled with horse-drawn refugee carts."*

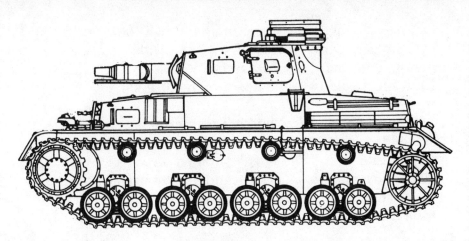

Panzers probed for weak spots in the Allied lines, and then plunged right through. Motorized infantry followed close behind, cutting phone lines and seizing key crossroads. Time and again, the Allies reacted too slowly.

France now discovered that to stop a mobile attack in open country you need a mobile defense. Communications broke down as commanders lost touch with their men in the field. In Paris, there was a numbed sense of shock and disbelief.

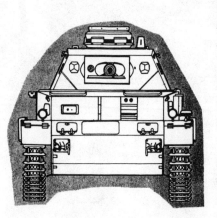

Hitler had yet another surprise. The Panzers bypassed Paris and pushed west to the English Channel. They suddenly swung north, capturing one port after the other. Churchill now realized that the Allied armies were about to be trapped in Belgium. And the only way out was a quaint seaside town named Dunkirk. It would take something like a miracle to save them now.

On May 25, the Panzers smashing through the defences of Dunkirk were ordered to halt. Hitler suddenly announced that *Reichsmarshal* Goering's glorious Luftwaffe would have the honor of the final kill.

This was the miracle Churchill was waiting for. Britain assembled a ragtag armada of 700 warships, tugs, and tiny private boats. The Royal Air Force flew cover while 200 thousand British troops and 130 thousand French were somehow rescued, despite constant pounding from the Luftwaffe. Here was the scene on the beaches:

"Abandoned vehicles, half sunk in the sand, fantastic twisted shapes of burned out skeletons and crazy-looking machinery heaped up in extraordinary piles by the explosion of bombs."

The British left nearly all their heavy guns, tanks, and other vehicles behind. But they lived to fight another day.

France would not be so lucky. The weary remnants of the French Army made a last, futile stand along the River Somme. The Germans attacked first one side of the line, then the other, looking for an opening. After days of fierce fighting, the Panzers finally forced a gap and plunged through. Panic spread like an epidemic. A French officer remembered the deep fear and shame:

"The flood of limping soldiers trying to look like men in the presence of the fleeing women... The whole disordered funeral procession of a disintegrating army."

This was the moment, June l0, when Mussolini finally found the courage to declare war on France and England. The Rome-Berlin **Axis** had become a military reality. And even though most Italians wanted peace, Il Duce had other plans:

"To make a people great it is necessary to send them to battle, even if you have to kick them in the pants."

On June ll, Paris was declared an Open City. Three days, later the capital fell without a shot. Triumphant German troops hung a giant Swastika from the *Arc de Triomphe* and goose-stepped down the *Champs Elysees*.

Meanwhile, two million Parisians clogged the roads, desperate for escape. President Reynaud and the rest of the French government fled to safety in the south. On June 16 — just five weeks after the German invasion — France surrendered.

Marshal Henri Petain was summoned to form a new government. He was an 84 year old veteran of the First World War, and the hero of the battle of Verdun. Stately, pompous, conservative, and vain, Petain agreed to engineer the process of capitulation:

"I make to France the gift of my person to help to mitigate her suffering."

Nazi peace terms were severe. France would pay billions in reparations and send millions of French workers to slave in the factories of the Reich. Worse, the northern two-thirds of France would be occupied by Germany.

In the south, Petain was allowed to install a puppet government at the spa town of Vichy. But the real decisions would be made by career politician Pierre Laval, who was only too eager to collaborate.

The formal French surrender was at Compiegne, in the same railroad car where Germany had signed the Armistice that ended the First World War. American news correspondent, William Shirer, saw Hitler's face "afire with scorn, anger, hate, revenge, triumph."

France had surrendered, but not the French. From London came a call to resistance from a virtually unknown patriot who, at age 49, was the youngest general in the Army. A longtime advocate of mobile warfare, he had commanded a small tank unit before the collapse – when he was ordered to escape to Britain. Now **Charles de Gaulle** spoke on the radio for the first time:

"To all Frenchmen, France has lost a battle. But France has not lost the war."

The Battle of France was over. But the Battle of Britain was just about to begin.

Britain stood alone. After the loss of her tanks and heavy guns at Dunkirk, she was practically defenseless. It seemed as if only the narrow waters of the English Channel could protect her now. The only question was for how long?

Hitler always assumed that the island nation would make peace as soon as the French were knocked out of the war. The British, after all, were known as a reasonable people, temperate, level-headed. Now the Fuehrer learned that his enemy had another side: steady and tenacious as a bulldog when aroused:

"Since England, in spite of her militarily hopeless situation, shows no sign of coming to terms, I have decided to prepare a landing ... and, if necessary, to carry it out."

"We shall fight them on the beaches, we shall fight them on the landing grounds, we shall fight them in the fields and in the streets, we shall fight in the hills. We shall never surrender."

During these dark days, it was Prime Minister **Winston Churchill** who symbolized the very spirit of defiance. Local militia drilled with pitchforks, sticks, and World War I rifles. Gas masks were distributed. The ringing of church bells would announce the inevitable enemy landings.

The German High Command drew up ambitious plans for **Operation SeaLion**. The Nazi invasion would combine air attacks, paratroop drops, and a major amphibious assault across the treacherous waters of the Channel. But first the plucky Royal Air Force —the **RAF**— had to be driven from the skies.

Goering bragged that he could finish the job in a few weeks. The Luftwaffe had 1200 bombers and 1000 frontline fighters to throw into the battle. On paper, estimated RAF strength was down to a mere 450 warplanes.

The real situation in the air was quite different, though. After Dunkirk, Churchill had made fighter aircraft his top industrial priority. In a single month of feverish activity, British factories doubled RAF fighter strength to 900 planes. Now for the first time, Germany would have to face an enemy on something like equal terms.

Plus, the swift British Spitfires were just as good as Hitler's *Messerschmitts*, and the young English pilots flying them were well-trained, seasoned, and spoiling for a fight. Also in Britain's favor was a new invention called **radar.** In the great battle to come, antennas strung along the coast would give advance warning of enemy attack and let the RAF concentrate its limited forces.

On **Eagle Day,** August 10, 1940, Goering sent 1,000 planes to attack RAF bases and aircraft factories all over England. From deep in the underground headquarters of British Fighter Command, the first enemy aircraft were tracked on radar. The order was given to **scramble**. In moments, hundreds of RAF pilots were airborne:

"It was each man for himself. As soon as they saw us they spread out and dived, and the next ten minutes was a blur of twisting machines and tracer bullets."

"Then I was pulling out, so hard that I could feel my eyes dropping through my neck. Coming around in a slow climbing turn, I saw that we had broken them up."

The Spits and the older British Hurricanes slipped through the German fighter screen to slash at the enemy's vulnerable bombers. In the early fighting, the Luftwaffe was badly bloodied. Yet the Germans kept pounding away at the RAF. Slowly, Goering began to win the battle of attrition.

Day after day—sometimes 3, 4, and even 5 times a day—RAF pilots would return after dogfighting "Gerry" to find their airfields pitted with bomb craters. A few moments to bolt down some food, refuel and rearm, and then they were off again. After weeks of this strain, British Fighter Command was close to the breaking point.

Then the Nazis made a fatal mistake. On the night of August 24, several German bombers missed a military target and dropped their bomb load on London for the first time in the war. In retaliation, Churchill ordered attacks on Berlin. He was hoping to goad Hitler into making a strategic blunder which might take the heat off the RAF. And that is exactly what happened.

"We will raze their cities to the ground."

On September 7, 1940, it is finally London's turn to feel the full fire of the Blitz. The sudden, eerie wail of air raid sirens fills the blacked-out streets as dozens of powerful floodlights probe the sky. Then, from a distance, comes the low drone of enemy airplanes approaching.

Night explodes with the sound of anti-aircraft guns pumping explosive shells high into the air. Overhead, hundreds of shiny airborne specks with wings inch into view, caught like bugs in the glare of floodlights. The planes seemed to hover in midair just long enough to drop their load: half-ton bombs that look no more threatening than black marbles falling from a child's silver toy.

Moments later, there's a strange whistling sound overhead, like a tea kettle gone berserk. The night explodes with a flash brighter than lightning and the sidewalk trembles. Smoke and the smell of burning brick fill the air. As the roar increases, bombs seem to creep ever forward, block by block, house by house, thundering like the hobnail boots of an angry giant. Soon the whole city is a smoking battleground.

Many Londoners sought refuge in the city's Underground train stations.

"We heard this terrible crash. We all ran out to see. It was this Woolworth's and all these kiddies' bodies were brought out. They had cardboard coffins. We made so many, but we never made enough."

"Please God, if you're going to kill us with these bombs, let's all die together, at night."

"This misery of that wretched mass of humanity sleeping like worms packed in a tin — the heat and the smell, the dirt, the endless crying of the poor bloody babies..."

"Sometimes a thousand a night came over, in waves. We had a saying, 'I'm gonna getcha, I'm gonna getcha.' That's how the planes sounded."

70

In the midst of the rubble, soldiers and firemen fought the flames and desperately searched for survivors. For three full months the Blitz continued — devastating whole areas of London, Coventry, Bristol, and Glasgow. Thousands died; ten times that number were left homeless. But the terror failed to shatter the morale of the British. Some were even able to see humor in the midst of destruction.

With the pressure off their bases, the RAF steadily gained the upper hand in the air. By January of 1941, the Battle of Britain seemed all but over. Germany had lost 1733 planes, England 915. While the Luftwaffe had been bled white, the RAF was actually getting stronger by the day.

"Never before in the course of human conflict, was so much owed by so many to so few."

Hitler was now forced to postpone Operation Sea Lion indefinitely. Goering had been shamed. And it was Winston Churchill who flashed the **V for Victory** sign and eloquently gave the men and women of the Royal Air Force the tribute they deserved.

If Britain couldn't be bombed into submission, perhaps it could be starved. The Nazis knew the island nation depended on supplies shipped from overseas for its industry and very survival. Cut those lifelines and Britain would be powerless.

Britannia still ruled the waves, but under the waves German submarines reigned supreme. Each week, dozens of British merchant vessels were sunk by the deck guns or torpedoes of enemy subs. In October 1940, Nazi Undersea Boats or *U-Boats* reached the peak of their deadly proficiency. If things continued, England would lose a third of her entire merchant fleet within a year.

The Royal Navy was stretched thin. Large forces had to be kept close to Britain to guard against invasion. To protect the transport convoys, Chuchill needed swift destroyers to tackle the U-Boats on their own terms. For help, he turned to an old ally, the United States.

America was officially neutral in the European war. The USA was recovering from the ravages of the Great Depression. Millions were still out of work. Few wanted to get involved overseas. Even President **Franklin Delano Roosevelt** tried to run as a peace candidate in the election of 1940. His slogan was: *He kept us out of war.*

"We cannot escape danger or the fear of danger by crawling into bed and pulling the covers over our eyes... A nation can have peace with the Nazis only at the price of surrender."

But the fall of France changed things. With England now standing alone against Nazi tyranny, FDR and millions of other Americans were forced to reconsider America's policy of isolationism.

Roosevelt was opposed by an influential group of isolationists called **America First**. They believed that powerful "Fortress America" could defend the hemisphere without getting involved in Europe. Isolationist hero **Charles Lindbergh**, the first man to fly the Atlantic, had visited Hitler's Germany in the late 1930's, and was deeply impressed by Nazi order and discipline. Now he warned America that Hitler was invincible.

"**America for Americans.**"

Other supporters of America First were rightwing conservatives who admired Hitler and shared his racial views – especially about Jews.

A genuine Nazi front, the **German American Bund**, campaigned for the creation of a white Anglo-Saxon Reich in North America. These bigots denounced the man they called Franklin Delano *Rosenfeld* and the Jewish bankers who supposedly controlled him. Their slogan appealed to racists of all nationalities.

FDR weathered the storm. In August 1940, at the height of the Blitz, Roosevelt pushed through Congress a bill which permitted the trade of 50 obsolete World War I naval destroyers to Britain. In return, Churchill transfered ownership of several Caribbean islands to be used as US bases.

The following month, Congress created the first American peacetime draft in history. More than a million men received letters of **Greetings** from their draftboards. They showed up at hastily-constructed army bases around the country. Here they trained with wooden rifles and cardboard tanks. But within months, they would have all the weapons a revitalized US industry could provide.

Finally in December, 1940, FDR got approval for **Lend Lease**. America would become what Roosevelt called "the great arsenal of democracy." Churchill could now buy billions of dollars worth of US arms and supplies on credit. And this meant that England could go on fighting—even though its treasury was empty.

With US help, Britain had survived its darkest hour. Now Churchill began to hit back. In North Africa, a small British tank force led the attack against a half million Italian troops massed in Libya. They crossed the desert by night to surprise the Fascists from the rear.

Mussolini's army panicked and ran, leaving behind most of their equipment. Tens of thousands surrendered. The Fascist fortress of Tobruk fell on January 21, 1941, yielding another 30,000 Italian prisoners of war. It was only then that Hitler took action.

For Germany, the Mediterranean was a sideshow to the real war. Yet Hitler realized that Mussolini's dictatorship might not survive the shame of a total defeat in Africa. To bolster the Axis cause, the Fuehrer sent a small mechanized force to Tripoli under the command of a promising German tank commander, already famous for his speed and daring: **General Erwin Rommel.**

On **May 10 1941,** the Luftwaffe staged its last major terror attack against London. Nearly 700 acres of the city were set ablaze. Every single church in the center of town was damaged or destroyed. The Tower of London, Parliament, and Westminster Abbey were all targeted. Even Big Ben suffered a hit, but the great clock — like the hearts of the English — failed to miss even a single beat.

After Goering's final show of strength, Hitler shifted the Luftwaffe far to the East. It was here, on the border with Russia, that the fate of the world would soon be decided.

Chapter V: BARBAROSA

The Battle of Britain was Germany's first defeat. Like a shark, Hitler knew that he must keep moving. Attack was everything. His mind turned from the watery tanktrap of the English Channel to the wide open plains of Russia. It was here, as he had predicted in *Mein Kampf*, that Germany would find its ultimate lebensraum.

The German-Soviet Nonaggression Pact had always been just a marriage of convenience. Now Hitler wanted a divorce.

He also desired Russia's riches: the wheat of the Ukraine, the coal of the Donetz, the oil of the Caucasus. Germany needed these resources to carry on the war and feed the ambitions of the Master Race. In December 1940, the Fuehrer gave this order to his generals:

"The German armed forces must be prepared, even before the conclusion of war against England, to crush Soviet Russia in a rapid campaign."

The generals protested feebly. A two-front war was every German's nightmare. Yet Hitler insisted that the mighty Wehrmacht could quickly destroy Stalin's Red Army, occupy European Russia, and then turn on the English. For luck, the battle plan was named after a great Teutonic warlord who carved out an empire in the east, **Barbarosa**.

The invasion was supposed to begin promptly on May 15, 1941. But events took a different course. On March 26, the pro-German regime in Yugoslavia was suddenly overthrown.

Like a frustrated child, Hitler ordered the total destruction of Yugoslavia "with merciless brutality." Powerful Panzer forces were shifted away from the Soviet border for an immediate invasion. On April 16, Belgrade was bombarded by the Luftwaffe. Armored units quickly followed, subduing the small nation by April 17.

Greece was next. The Greeks, supported by a small detatchment of British troops, had shamed Mussolini by crushing a large Italian invasion in the mountains of the north. Now Hitler's Panzers easily broke through the Allied lines. Churchill hastily evacuated his troops and tried to dig in on nearby Crete. But a daring German paratrooper landing took the strategic island by storm.

Yet the cost of victory came high. The invasion of Russia had to be delayed for six long weeks. Finally, on June 22, 1941, everything was at last back in place. It was just one day later than the date that Napoleon had also tried the same thing in the year 1812. Still, the average German soldier was confident:

"In the distance you can hear muffled rumbles of the front, planes are flying overhead, and we lie in the sunlit grass under high trees and wait for our call."

It was the Blitzkrieg all over again – only on a far grander scale. The Luftwaffe surprised 2,000 Soviet planes on the ground and destroyed them in the first hours of the morning. Then came the familiar pattern of dive bombers and artillery smashing holes in enemy defence, followed by swift columns of Panzers. The Red Army was caught completely off guard. Total chaos reigned in the Russian lines.

"We are being fired on. What shall we do?"

It took four hours for Soviet headquarters to finally give the order to shoot back at the enemy. Stalin was in total shock. Churchill and even Roosevelt, a neutral, had warned him of Hitler's invasion plans. Stalin's own agents reported the massing of nearly four million German troops along the frontier of occupied Poland. Yet the usually-paranoid Soviet dictator stubbornly refused to believe that Hitler would stab **him** in the back. Now his nation would pay the price.

Worse, Stalin's bloody purges had robbed the Red Army of its best officers. Basic military strategy had been ignored. Millions of Soviet troops were spread out along the vast frontier in exposed positions. In the first days of fighting, hundreds of thousands of Russians were killed or captured, thousands of tanks destroyed.

Three weeks passed before the Red dictator addressed his terrified nation over the radio. To survive, Stalin told the Soviet people that they would have to create a desert of **scorched earth** in front of the invader:

"The enemy must not find a single railway engine, not a wagon, not a pound of bread, or a glassful of petrol."

The Panzers continued to roll forward at great speed, time and again turning inward to trap the hapless Russians. In the first month, the Wehrmacht had captured Smolensk, two-thirds of the way to Moscow. A million Soviet prisoners were now behind barbed wire. And the Germans were still very much on the move. But in which direction?

Hitler now split his forces. One powerful Army sped north to encircle Leningrad. The other swept south into the Ukraine, Russia's rich breadbasket. Kiev, the Ukrainian capital, was surrounded and captured on September l9th — together with 600,000 Soviet troops.

Russia seemed to be collapsing. Half of the massive Red Army was dead, wounded, or captured. Only 700 tanks remained of its original 15,000. Yet even as the Soviets gave up ground, they kept fighting. German supply lines now stretched many hundreds of miles. Wehrmacht commanders began to worry:

"The spaces seemed endless... We were depressed by the monotony of the landscape, the immensity of forest marsh, and plain...."

In faraway Berlin, the view was different. Easy victories had led Hitler to underestimate Stalin and the army of *subhumans* fighting under the Red Flag. The Fuehrer now ordered his troops to switch directions and march on Moscow. The Kremlin, he smugly predicted, would be in his hands long before the arrival of Winter.

This prediction almost came true. By mid-October, the Germans were only 200 miles from the Soviet capital. Muscovites began to flee the city in terror. Yet now Stalin refused to panic. He stayed in the Kremlin, and he finally placed a first rate commander in charge of his troops: General Georgi Zhukov.

The Blitzkrieg days of summer turned into the torrents of the autumn. Mud filled the roads. German troops became exhausted by the effort to push forward and fight at the same time. Yet Hitler kept insisting that the Nazi will to victory was more powerful than any obstacle. As the drive on Moscow slowed to a crawl, Panzer General Heinz Guderian wrote in his combat diary:

"We have seriously under-estimated the Russians, the extent of the country, and the treachery of the climate. This is the revenge of reality."

Now the Germans would meet their ultimate enemy: **General Winter.**

At the end of October, temperatures suddenly dropped. The roads froze, and the Panzers were able to advance again toward Moscow. But it soon grew even colder. On November 12, the thermometer read -10° Fahrenheit; on December 4, it sank to -31°.

The Germans had not prepared for a long winter campaign. Their weapons jammed in the intense cold. There was was no antifreeze for their vehicles. Fires had to be built under trucks to start them. Tanks were kept running day and night to keep their engines from freezing solid. Bad weather often grounded the Luftwaffe.

Out in the open, soldiers simply froze. Hitler refused to supply adequate clothing – since he planned to have the troops back home, victorious, by Christmas. By the first week of December, 100,000 German troops had already been hospitalized for frostbite. A disillusioned medical officer made this report:

"In the unearthly cold, in which icicles hung from nostrils and eyelashes all day long, where thinking became an effort, the German soldier fought no longer for an ideal or an ideology, no longer for the Fatherland. They fought blindly without asking questions, without wanting to know what lay ahead."

On December 5, 1941, the Germans fought their way into the suburbs of Moscow. They were heartened by the sight of searchlights and antiaircraft shells flashing high above the Kremlin, now less than 25 miles away. But they could go no further.

On December 6, Stalin ordered a massive counter-attack. He threw into battle 20 fresh divisions—rushed by rail from Siberia—completely outfitted for winter fighting. And this time it was the Germans who gave ground.

Hitler would never admit any personal role in failure. Over the radio, he told the German people that unpatriotic elements in the Army had sabotaged the Russian campaign. He cruelly humiliated and then dismissed many of the Wehrmacht's ablest commanders. Then he announced that commanding the troops in the field was "a little affair" anyone could do. As a result, he was taking personal control of the armed forces.

"The Commander-in-Chief's job is to train the Army in the National Socialist idea. And I know of no General who could do that as I want it done."

Adolf Hitler now ran the Nazi Party, the German Government, the General Staff of the Army, as well as the High Command of the Armed Forces. In coming battles, he would even assume command over the day-to-day affairs of individual units on the battlefield. All of this he would accomplish hundreds of miles away from the Front -- at his wartime headquarters called the **Wolf's Lair**, deep in the grim forest solitude of East Prussia.

With Russia suddenly in the war, England was no longer alone. Churchill eagerly embraced an alliance with Stalin -- a man about whom he had no illusions:

"If Hitler invaded Hell, I should at least make a favorable reference to the Devil in the House of Commons."

Britain had to keep Russia in the war at all costs. Churchill shipped Stalin a large part of the weapons pouring out of British factories -- as well as much of the Lend Lease supplies arriving from America. What began as a trickle, soon became a torrent that help turn the tides of war.

In just two years, the conflict had expanded from a border conflict between Germany and Poland to a struggle involving the whole of Europe. Halfway around the globe, in Asia, stormclouds now threatened to bring the rest of the world into the fight.

Chapter VI

The Rising Sun

In 1941, Imperial Japan was on the march. The island nation had been at war with a weak, divided China for nearly a decade. Would America risk war to stop the spread of Japanese might throughout Asia?

It was not the first time these Pacific powers had faced off against each other. Back in 1853, an American fleet under command of Commodore Matthew Perry sailed uninvited into Tokyo Harbor. The nation was to be opened to international trade -- whether it liked it or not.

Japan had been closed to foreign influences for centuries. Even firearms had been banned, since they threatened the power of the island's noble families and their private armies of *samurai* swordsmen. Yet now all Japanese were forced to accept that the modern age had dawned in **Nippon,** the Land of the Rising Sun.

Here life had always been hard. The islands forming Japan are extremely mountainous, with little open land for farming. Frequent earthquakes and constant wars made existence precarious. Perhaps for these reasons, the Japanese evolved a unique culture — with an original way of looking at life and death.

Shinto, the ancient folk cult of the islands, stressed the links between the present and the past, the living and the dead. Respect for one's ancestors was as necessary and natural as obedience to one's superiors here on earth.

Buddhism, arriving later from China, stressed that life and death were illusions. Eternity could be glimpsed in an instant, in the fall of cherry blossoms or the ripple of moonlight on the waters.

Yet this very traditional people was able to industrialize and change more rapidly than anyone could've imagined. Within 40 years after Perry's visit, Japan had become a master of the art of modern warfare. In 1894, Imperial forces went to war against China. Victory was swift. The Chinese were humiliated, and forced to hand over Taiwan and part of northern China.

In 1904, the Imperial fleet boldly launched a sneak attack on the Russian navy based at Port Arthur, in nearby Manchuria. Triumphant Japanese ground and naval forces proved for the first time that Asians could defeat Westerners armed with modern weapons. As part of victory, Japan annexed neighboring Korea.

During World War I, Japan joined the Allied side, and was rewarded with German colonial rights in Shantung, northern China. Japanese influence soon spread throughout Manchuria. But Imperial leaders began dreaming of even greater glory. In 1927, Prime Mininster Tanaka laid out the basic strategy for world conquest:

"...Under the pretense of trade and commerce, penetrate the rest of China. Having China's entire resources at our disposal, we shall proceed to conquer India...Asia Minor, Central Asia, and even Europe."

In 1932, Tokyo seized Manchuria outright, creating the puppet state of *Manchukuo*. Enraged Chinese attacked Japanese and other foreigners in the cosmopolitan coastal city of Shanghai. In response, the Imperial Air Force ruthlessly bombed that city for six weeks. Japan responded to international criticism by withdrawing from the League of Nations.

Yet there were influential liberal forces in Tokyo that still favored peace and economic — not military — expansion. In February 1936, Nationalist fanatics in the Imperial Army rose up in revolt against them. Many high civilian leaders were assassinated. From now on, Japan would be dominated by soldiers.

By 1938, Japan had found one pretext or another to attack and occupy Peking, Shanghai, Canton, and Nanking. Millions of Chinese fled Japanese brutalities. Even President Chiang Ki-shek was forced to move his capital far inland to Chungking. In this undeclared war, America still maintained official neutrality.

Yet President Roosevelt didn't object when a volunteer air force was sent to China to fight. Japanese airmen soon learned to fear the pilots of the Flying Tigers, under the command of retired US General Claire Chennault.

The balance of power was now rapidly tilting toward Japan. Washington tried to use economic pressure to force Japanese withdrawl from Indochina. On August 11, 1941, America united with Britain to block the shipment of oil to Japan. Soon other essential war materials, such as rubber, steel, and strategic minerals, were also banned.

In Tokyo, the weakened Peace party, led by Prince Kinoye, favored a diplomatic solution. War with America would be a disaster, they insisted. The US had twice Japan's population. And it's industrial base was nearly six times as great.

In 1940, Tokyo joined fellow militarists in Germany and Italy to become the eastern pole of the **Axis Powers**. After the fall of France, Imperial troops quickly moved in to occupy the large French colony of Indochina—Vietnam, Laos and Cambodia.

The War Party, led by Army leader **General Hideki Tojo**, replied that a shameful withdrawal might lead to another bloody Army revolt. Yet even as the debate continued, the fact remained that Japan's strategic supply of oil was rapidly dwindling.

Tojo used the tense situation to become Prime Minister. Talks with Washington were continued. And they continued to go nowhere. On November 26, the USA upped its demands. It now demanded that Japan withdraw from China, Indochina, and Axis Alliance.

Did FDR really think Tojo would back down? Or was he trying to goad Tokyo into military actions that would finally bring America into the war? A half century later, historians still debate this question. What we do know is that on November 27, Navy Secretary Knox sent this dire warning to US forces throughout the Pacific:

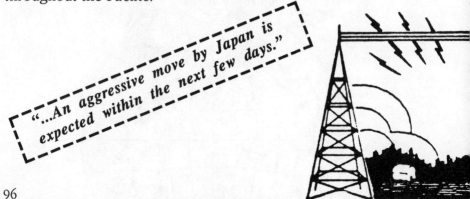

"...An aggressive move by Japan is expected within the next few days."

America had cracked the secret Japanese code. Roosevelt knew that Tojo planned an attack somewhere. But where? US strategy was to use naval forces based in Hawaii to repell attacks on US bases in the Philippines or Midway island. No one imagined that the Japanese would ever dare to strike the mighty Pacific fleet itself, moored at Pearl Harbor. This attack was the product of a brilliant military mind: Japanese **Admiral Isoroku Yamamoto.** He predicted that a sneak attack could result in a string of Japanese victories lasting perhaps six months. But after that, a great disaster loomed ahead:

"I warn you, if hostilities continue for two or three years, then I have no confidence that ultimate victory will be ours."

Yamamoto's prophecy was quickly forgotten as planning for the airstrike continued. On November 26, the day of the US ultimatum, a powerful Japanese strike force left port. It boasted six powerful aircraft carriers, with a complement of 423 planes, including bombers and torpedo bombers.

On December 6, Japanese diplomats in Washington sent a final message to Tokyo, reporting no progress in negotiations with the US government. Now there could be no turning back.

On the morning of December 7, 1941, at 6:00AM, the first wave of Imperial torpedo bombers was launched in the direction of Hawaii, 275 miles away.

US radar picked up a large force of approaching aircraft. But it was assumed they were just a flight of American B-l7 bombers arriving from California. The first enemy dive bombers struck an hour later:

"Pearl Harbor was still asleep in the morning mist. It was calm and serene inside the harbor, not even a trace of smoke from the ships at Oahu."

"The battleship appeared to leap suddenly into view across the front of my machine looking huge like a vast gray mountain... standby! Fire!"

"Air raid, Pearl Harbor — this is no drill."

A second wave of bombers attacked at 8:40 a.m. In less than two hours, the Japanese crippled most of the US Pacific Fleet. Two battleships, the *Arizona* and the *Oklahoma*, sank almost immediately; battleships *West Virginia* and *California* soon followed. Another four battleships were badly damaged. Three cruisers and a number of smaller ships were also sent to the bottom.

Most of the island's air defenses were knocked out on the ground – a total of 108 bombers and fighters. Altogether, 3,453 US soldiers, sailors, marines, and civilians died in the attack. Of the Japanese planes in the operation, only 29 were shot down.

The miracle was that none of the four aircraft carriers in the fleet was at Pearl when the attack began. Most US submarines were also out on maneuvers and escaped destruction. This meant that America still had in its arsenal the two most decisive weapons of modern naval warfare. Soon Tokyo would feel their power.

A grim President Roosevelt spoke to America over the radio:

"Yesterday, December 7, a day which will live in infamy – the United States of America was suddenly and deliberately attacked by naval and air forces of the Empire of Japan."

It was war! Americans were shocked and enraged. Wild hysteria swept the West Coast. Enemy subs and imaginary landings were reported everywhere. The US Government quickly rounded up 100,000 Japanese-Americans and penned them in desolate detention camps far from their homes. Anti-Asian racism was now at its peak.

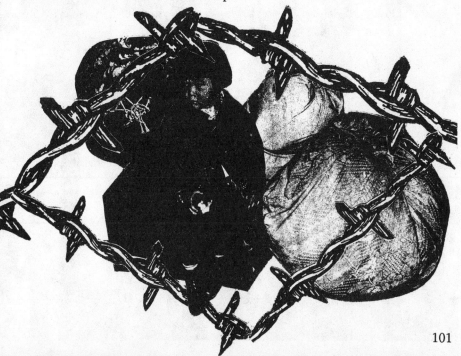

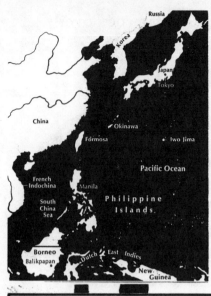

Tokyo now struck the American base in the Philippines. On December 8—despite warnings—most of the US Far Eastern Air Force was destroyed on the ground. An invasion force of 57,000 Imperial troops soon came ashore only 120 miles from the capital of Manila. The Yanks defending the islands were still reeling in shock.

"We were Americans, they were Japanese...We were always told that they all wore glasses and they didn't have a decent bombsight. And they didn't have any navy to amount to anything... Jesus Christ, how the hell'd this happen?"

By January 6, the 30,000 American troops in the area were ordered to withdraw to a defensible peninsula in the south of Luzon. It was only 25 miles long by 20 miles wide. Its terrain was rugged, covered with mountains, jungle, and mosquito-filled swamps. And it was known by the name of **Bataan**.

Here the Yanks dug in and waited for help that never came. Food and ammunition were in short supply. Malaria and dysentery swept through the ranks. The hard-pressed men on Bataan were on their own.

Brutal fighting went on for months. On March 10, President Roosevelt ordered General Douglas **MacArthur** to escape by torpedo boat to Australia. There he would take command of all Allied ground forces in the Pacific. Before he left, the General swore:

"I shall return."

This promise seemed far off. On April 9 1942, the last Americans fighting in Bataan finally surrendered. Yet just across a two-mile strait, 15,000 Yanks still clung to the island bastion of **Corregidor** – a heavily armed fortress dug deep into solid rock.

On May 4, enemy bombardment of over 16,000 shells prepared the way for invasion. Next day, both armies fought hand to hand on the beaches. The Yanks were slowly forced back into their protective tunnels. Here is one of the last radio messages from embattled Corregidor:

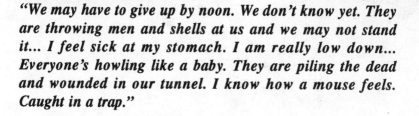

"We may have to give up by noon. We don't know yet. They are throwing men and shells at us and we may not stand it... I feel sick at my stomach. I am really low down... Everyone's howling like a baby. They are piling the dead and wounded in our tunnel. I know how a mouse feels. Caught in a trap."

The trap was worse than they imagined. The following day, General Jonathan Wainwright, acting commander of remaining US forces in the Philippines, gave his men the order to surrender. But Japan did not feel bound by the international Geneva Convention accord for humane treatment of prisoners of war (POWs). Under the warrior's code of *Bushido*, a soldier who laid down his arms shamed himself, his family, and the divine Emperor.

Soldiers who surrendered – even under direct orders – deserved only abuse. And that's exactly what the Imperial Army gave them on the **Bataan Death March**:

"I heard a cry, followed by thudding blows... An American soldier so tortured by thirst that he could not sleep had asked a guard for water. The Jap fell on him with his fists, then slugged him into insensibility with a rifle."

"The Japanese emptied out the hospitals. Anybody that could walk they forced them into line... If you fell out to the side, you were either shot by the guards, or you were bayoneted and left there."

The survivors found conditions little better in the prison camps that would be their home for the next three years. Malaria, disease, overwork, brutality—and always hunger.

An equally brutal fate awaited tens of thousands of British soldiers and civilians—men, women, and children—when the Japanese seized Hong Kong and the "invincible" fortress of Singapore from the rear. At Singapore, like the Maginot Line, the big defensive guns pointed in only one direction. The wrong one.

In six months, Japan had firmly established its **Co-Prosperity Sphere** over half of China, all of Indochina, Malaya, Burma, the Philippines, and the strategic oil fields of the Dutch East Indies. Only Australia, the last Allied stronghold, remained free. Would America have enough time to turn the tide?

Chapter Seven

THE NEW ORDER

The world has long known the horrors of war. What the Nazis taught the vanquished were the horrors of peace.

On New Year's Day 1942, all was still quiet on the German home front. The occasional Allied bombing raid was a nuisance; and it was sad to watch the young men go off to the Army. But there was food and drink, concerts and films aplenty. Life went on.

Not so in Nazi-occupied Europe. For millions life had become hell. Hitler's **new order** divided the world into masters and slaves.

Germans and other Northern Europeans were *übermenschen* – supermen. The French and all Latins were somewhat lower on the evolutionary scale. On the bottom, were the great mass of *untermenschen* – subhumans. These included Slavs, Jews, Arabs, Orientals, and Africans. Here's how the fanatical Nazis of the S.S. described the typical subhuman:

"His features resemble man, but intellectually, spiritually, he is lower than an animal."

Hitler commanded Poland to disappear. The first step was to liquidate the local elite. Thousands of doctors, lawyers, teachers, businessmen, government officials, journalists, and priests were jailed, sent to work camps, or simply taken out and shot. Polish schools, museums, libraries, and theatres were closed. To limit the biological potential of these Slavs, rations were to be kept at bare subsistence levels. S.S. leader Heinrich Himmler believed his slaves should be allowed to learn simple arithmetic up to 500, the ability to write their name, and a doctrine that it is divine law to obey the Germans.

In Western Europe, the New Order was achieved by more civilized, but no less effective, means. France was forced to pay ten times the real cost of German occupation. For the French, this meant malnutrition and shortages. For the Reich it was a way to obtain raw materials, food, and manufactured goods at no expense.

Reichsmarshal Goering amassed an incredible personal fortune. His agents confiscated jewels, gold, and property in every occupied country – including priceless oil paintings *acquired* from French museums and shipped to his vast estate in the Reich.

> *"In the old days, the rule was plunder. Now, outward forms have become more humane. Nevertheless, I intend to plunder, and plunder copiously."*
>
> –Goering

109

The invasion of Russia opened up vast new vistas for plunder. The S.S. took over 1.5 million acres and ran them as vast plantations, using forced labor. Food was shipped to the Reich, while millions of Russian prisoners of war and civilians were slowly starved to death.

"We are a Master nation which must consider that racially and biologically, the least German is a thousand times more valuable than the local population."

Millions of helpless men and women were rounded up and forced to labor in factories and farms. German big business made rich profits renting workers directly from the S.S. And as long as the supply of prisoners seemed limitless, they could be treated even worse than slaves. A doctor visiting a factory near Nuremberg was shocked to discover the female prisoners suffering from festering wounds and other diseases. They had no shoes and went around barefoot, with their hair shorn.

As many as 7 million slave laborers were eventually deported to the Reich. Their sacrifice kept the German standard of living unusually high throughout the war. Allied prisoners of war were also forced, against the terms of the Geneva Convention, to work in munitions factories and stone quarries under dangerous and inhumane conditions:

"Employment must be in the true meaning of the word, exhaustive...There is no limit to working hours."

An even worse fate awaited the 8 million Jews caught in the Nazi trap. Persecution had begun with the Nazi takeover in 1933. At the 1935 Party Rally in Nuremburg, Hitler announced that Jews were deprived of their citizenship and all basic human rights. Soon marriage and sexual relations between Aryans and Jews was punishable by death.

Germany became a vast torture chamber for its half million Jews. Jews had to wear a yellow star or risk imprisonment and death. They were not allowed to own various shops or factories, enter certain Berlin streets, visit a museum, attend a concert or movie, own a pet, drive a car, sit on a park bench, use public transportation, possess a radio, buy a newspaper, or obtain the usual food rations. Bank accounts were seized. Over 400 anti-Jewish laws were decreed in Germany alone.

Then on November 8, 1938, an angry Jewish youth assassinated the German ambassador in Paris. Hitler ordered thousands of synagogues put to the torch. Jewish shops were smashed and looted. Broken glass filling the street gave this shameful event its name: **Krystalnacht** .

While police looked the other way, Brownshirts killed hundreds of Jews in cold blood. Nearly 30,000 were arrested and trucked off to the oblivion of concentration camps.

In 1939, these persecuted people became convenient scapegoats for the invasion of Poland:

> *"The Jews are our destruction. They provoked and brought about this war."*
>
> — Goebbels

By 1941, the secret policemen of the **gestapo** were allowed to arrest suspected opponents of the regime and have them disappear without a trace into *Nacht und Nebel* — night and fog. Political opponents, pacifists, homosexuals, gypsies, Jehovah Witnesses, and Jews soon filled concentration camps throughout the Reich.

Thousands of Jews like Anne Frank went into hiding, often for years in dark attics or basements, under floorboards, behind false walls:

> *"Who has inflicted this upon us? Who has made us Jews different from all other peoples? Who has allowed us to suffer so terribly?"*

Other Jews were trapped behind barbed wire and walls topped with broken glass in specially designated area within cities – crowded, squalid ghettos. Within the walls of the Warsaw Ghetto alone, 50,000 starved to death in a single year on the official **monthly** ration of 2 pounds of bread, nine ounces of sugar, three and one half ounces of jam, and two ounces of fat. Here was the horror first-hand:

> *"To pass that wall was to enter into a new world utterly unlike anything that had ever been imagined....As we picked our way across the mud and rubble, the shadows of what had once been men and women flitted by us in pursuit of something or someone, their eyes blazing with some insane hunger...Children, every bone in their skeleton showing through their taut skin, played in heaps and swarms."*

GETTO

Millions of other Eastern European Jews were simply taken out and shot. By 1942, it was a common occurrence throughout Russia:

*"The people who had got off the trucks —
men, women, and children of all ages —
had to undress upon the order of an S.S.
man who carried a riding crop or dog
whip. They had to put down their clothes
in fixed places..."*

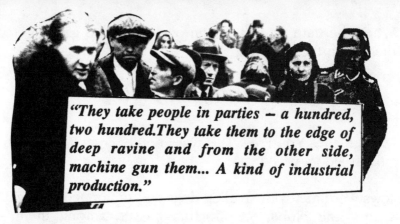

> *"They take people in parties — a hundred, two hundred. They take them to the edge of deep ravine and from the other side, machine gun them... A kind of industrial production."*

Yet even these methods were too slow and inefficient to satisfy the Nazis. Lethal experiments had already begun on Germans considered "useless mouths" — retarded children, the mentally disturbed, the incurables with anti-Nazi "delusions." Patients were slowly starved to death in hospitals. When a few brave ministers protested, more efficient disposal methods were introduced. These would soon be used on the Jews.

In 1941, at an estate just outside Berlin, Reinhard Heydrich of the S.S. told a group government and military leaders of the **Final Solution** to the Jewish problem: Death Camps with names like Bergen-Belsen, Ravensbruck, Mauthausen — and biggest of all — Auschwitz.

> *"The Germans said, You must take food for three days travel, clothes, and what you have of jewelry, gold and things."*

Victims were told they were being "resettled" in work camps further to the East. They were shoved into crowded railway cattlecars with little or no water, a bucket for a toilet. The journey could last days or even a week or more. Countless thousands died on the way.

When the train arrived, a sign over the camp gate greeted them with these words:

𝕬𝖗𝖇𝖊𝖎𝖙 𝕸𝖆𝖈𝖍𝖙 𝕱𝖗𝖊𝖎.

Work Makes You Free. This was another cruel lie. Here the only freedom was death.

Jews were met with snarling dogs and uniformed men with whips and clubs. S.S. doctors passed among them — making the Selection. With a flick of the finger, someone lived or died. Healthy young workers were sent in one direction. Most of the others aboard the transport — women, children, and elderly—were sent in the other. A rare survivor described what happened next:

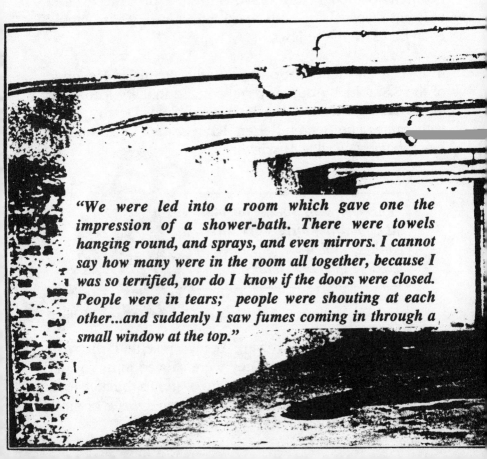

"We were led into a room which gave one the impression of a shower-bath. There were towels hanging round, and sprays, and even mirrors. I cannot say how many were in the room all together, because I was so terrified, nor do I know if the doors were closed. People were in tears; people were shouting at each other...and suddenly I saw fumes coming in through a small window at the top."

The fumes were Zyklon B poison gas, developed by **I.G. Farben**, a large, reputable German pharmaceutical company still in business today. After fifteen or twenty minutes, the victims were usually all dead. Then came the grisly task of processing the corpses. This was performed by other inmates, who would soon take their place in the gas chambers.

Nothing was wasted: hair for filling mattresses; gold and silver fillings from teeth for the Reichsbank; crushed bones for fertilizer; and at least in several camps, human fat for the manufacture of soap. The best clothing and personal effects, such as toothbrushes and eyeglasses, were sent back for distribution in Germany. According to official Auschwitz records, 99,992 articles of children's clothes, l92,625 pieces of women's underwear, and 222,269 pieces of men's underwear were made available in just six weeks.

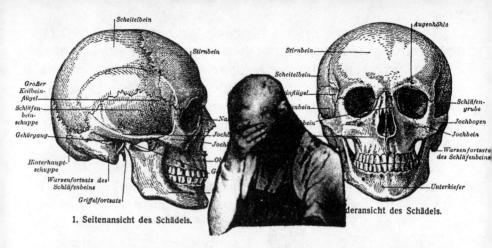

1. Seitenansicht des Schädels.

Dehumanization was the fate of those selected for work. Prisoners had their heads shaven and numbers tatooed on their arms. They were issued thin, tattered striped uniforms to wear summer and winter, and wooden clogs which bruised their feet. They were piled into drafty barracks, where sanitation was nearly nonexistent and where vermin and disease were everywhere.

The well-fed S.S. guards took every opportunity to torment the prisoners. Many inmates were simply beaten or kicked to death. Others were shot or hung. Still others had fiendish medical experiments performed on them by quack Nazi doctors.

Next to terror, hunger was the greatest torment. The day's ration was a hunk of bread, mostly parsnips and sawdust, and a watery soup made from turnips and even grass. Life expectancy was estimated at three to six months—even less when inmates were forced to slave away in rock quarries and mines underground.

When slave labor took its final toll on the body, there still awaited the ovens and chimneys of the crematoria – running night and day. The stench and smoke was a constant reminder of the inevitable.

Six million Jews died during the years of the Nazi New Order. They were joined by countless Poles, Russians, Czechs, gypsies, homosexuals, prisoners of war, religious objectors, and the captured heroes of the anti-Nazi Resistance.

To be sure, there were revolts. Inmates of Camps like **Treblinka** and **Sorbibor** rose up to kill their guards and escape. In **Auschwitz** itself, doomed prisoners used stolen dynamite to destroy a gas chamber, before trying to escape through the wire.

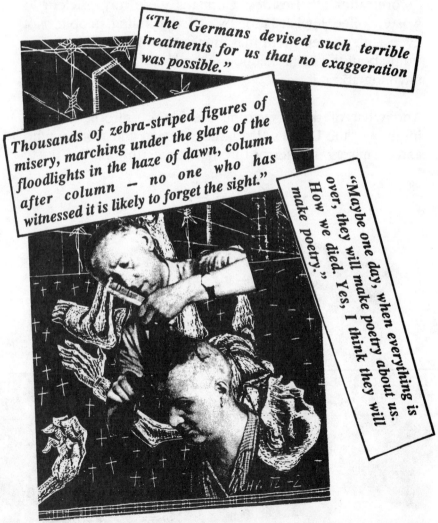

"The Germans devised such terrible treatments for us that no exaggeration was possible."

Thousands of zebra-striped figures of misery, marching under the glare of the floodlights in the haze of dawn, column after column — no one who has witnessed it is likely to forget the sight."

"Maybe one day, when everything is over, they will make poetry about us. How we died. Yes, I think they will make poetry."

Throughout Europe, Jews ran off to the forest or hills to join the partisans. Thousands in the Warsaw Ghetto fought to the death with a handful of weapons and gasoline bombs. Their desperate heroism forced the Nazis to spend weeks demolishing the Ghetto, block by block, by bombing and fire. As Hitler himself had said:

"When it comes to the Jews, I have no mercy."

Yet the majority of Jews were lulled into inaction by German propaganda. There had been persecutions before, after all. Besides, Germans were too efficient to waste skilled Jewish labor by actually killing people. Not even Hitler hated them that much. Most learned the tragic truth about the Final Solution when it was far too late to do anything about it.

And what of those wearing the black uniform and the insignia of the Death's Head, the S.S. men and women who spread misery and terror through this earthly hell?

Many S. S. men brought their wives and children to stay with them just outside the electrified wires that marked the boundaries of life and death. Here they lived like princes, tended by emaciated slaves in threadbare striped uniforms. Here they could be serenaded at Christmas concerts by tatooed virtuosi, and exchange gifts made in prison workshops by starving artisans doomed to the ashes. For all of this strange breed of humanity, Heinrich Himmler had a bizarre tribute:

"Most of you will know what it means to have seen 100 corpses together, or 500 or 1000. To have made one's way through that, and — some instances of human weakness aside — to have remained a decent person throughout, that is what has made us hard."

Yet even such unspeakable inhumanity could not win victory – once the tides of war finally turned.

Chapter VIII:
THE TIDE TURNS

Control of Europe was no longer the key to world conquest. Could the Berlin-Rome-Tokyo **Axis** defeat the combined population, productivity, and military strength of half the world?

After Pearl Harbor, America channeled its rage into war production. FDR announced plans to build an amazing 60,000 aircraft, 75,000 tanks, and millions of tons of merchant shipping per year. To meet these quotas, women across the country were lured from the home to the factory.

Rosie the Riveter was the role model for a new generation of females — tough, resourceful, yet somehow unmistakably feminine. Women workers helped feed, dress, and arm all 15 million US soldiers and sailors.

American productivity was also crucial to winning the Battle of the Atlantic. By November 1942, US shipyards began turning out more vessels than the enemy could sink. New warships and inventions such as *sonar*, which used sound waves to detect objects under water, began to turn the U-Boat from hunter to the hunted.

In November 1942, the tides of victory began to turn on land when the British Army won a decisive victory against one of its most resourceful foes: **General Erwin Rommel**. Rommel's motorized **Afrika Korps** had long kept the English off-balance and on the run across hundreds of desert miles. He was a master of surprise and deception who soon earned the name *The Desert Fox*.

> *"No admiral ever won a naval battle from shore."*

Desert warfare in North Africa was an ordeal. Temperatures sometimes rose above 110 degrees fahrenheit at noon, and dropped down to the low 40s at night. Yellow dust caked the men and fouled the engines of their vehicles. Water was more precious than food or ammunition. And then there were the insects.

By May of 1942, Rommel had pushed the British out of Libya nearly back to the Egyptian border. Churchill demanded a counter-attack. An immense strike force assembled at a place called Gazala, but the wily Rommel struck first. The Afrika Korps used speed and surprise to throw its more powerful enemy off balance. British tanks advanced into battle in small groups -- and were picked off by German guns. As usual, Rommel was right in the middle of the action:

The Allies withdrew. Rommel now used a brilliant manuever to storm the British bastion of Tobruk. The Panzers had already bypassed Tobruk — when they suddenly wheeled around and attacked from the rear. German guns and divebombers blasted a hole in the defensives. Tanks quickly pushed through. Within just 24 hours, Rommel had seized this strategic base, 35,000 Allied troops, and great stockpiles of supplies.

The fall of Tobruk turned the orderly English withdrawl from Gazala into a mad rout. The British finally rallied in a narrow, arid patch of ground between the Mediterranean and a rocky, impenetrable canyon called the Qattara Depression. This place would become the great battle-ground known to history as **El Alamein.**

A badly-shaken Churchill appointed a new field commander for North Africa: **Viscount Bernard Montgomery.** He was a cautious, capable general with more than a touch of public relations genius. To counter Rommel's mystique of invincibility, "Monty" affected a defiant, jaunty air that seemed contagious down through the ranks:

"Give me three weeks, and I can resist the Boche. Give me a month and I can chase him out of Africa."

At Alamein, Montgomery's forces dug into strong defensive positions while waiting for massive reinforcements of men and equipment now pouring in from both Britain and the US.

On July 1, 1942, Rommel again tried to hit the British before they were strong enough to attack. He wanted to slip south through the desert at night and surprise the enemy from behind. But with most of the Luftwaffe transferred to Russia, he moved blindly and slammed right into the enemy defenses. On July 4th, Rommel was forced to write in his diary:

"Things are, unfortunately, not going as we should like... Our strength is exhausted."

"Rommel, Rommel, Rommel. What else matters but beating him?"

Churchill demanded an attack. But Monty was determined to build up strength.

125

On October 23, 1942, British infantry advanced silently under moonlight through the Nazi minefields. Rommel happened to be far away in Germany on sick leave when the night erupted with the thunder of 1000 Allied guns. The bombardment was so heavy that the temporary German commander died of a heart attack in the front lines. When British armor finally broke through — it was the Afrika Korps' turn to panic and flee.

"I jumped out of the armored car and beneath the burning midday sun, ran as fast as I could ... It was a place of living death, of burning tanks, and smashed flak guns, without a living soul."

In the chaos, the German Second in Command was captured. Rommel arrived by plane to find a deteriorating situation. He quickly rallied his men and prepared for escape. But Hitler ordered the Afrika Korps to stand and fight — even under relentless enemy attack.

Not until November was the bloodied Afrika Korps finally allowed to begin its thousand mile dash to safety in Tunisia, only one step ahead of Montgomery. Nearly 60,000 Axis troops and most of Rommel's guns and tanks were lost along the way.

Soon there was another conquest to celebrate: **Operation Torch**. On November 8, Allied troops under the command of a still-obscure US general, **Dwight Eisenhower**—better known as *Ike*—began landing in North Africa: on the coasts of Morocco, Algeria, and Tunisia. These French colonies were run by the corrupt collaborationist government of Marshal Petain, installed by the Germans in the French town of Vichy.

The American soldiers were called **G.I.s** – for Government Issue. Most had been civilians just a year before, yet they quickly adapted themselves to modern warfare. Among them was an eccentric ex-calvary commander with a genius for handling tanks: **General George Patton.** He liked to brag that his men were more afraid of him than they were of the enemy. In battles to come, the troops would give him the nickname "Old Blood and Guts" – their blood and his guts.

> *"Gentlemen, tomorrow we attack. If we are not victorious, let none come back alive."*

Vichy French naval and land forces were quickly overcome. Soon 100,000 fresh Allied troops quickly came ashore.

It began to look more and more like Rommel was caught in a gigantic vise. The Desert Fox begged Hitler to withdraw from Tunisia. But the Fuehrer ordered:

> *"Hold fast, never retreat, hurl every gun and every man into the fray... You can show your troops no other way than that which leads to <u>victory or death</u>."*

This was the same mistake that would lead to total disaster in Russia. For it was here, far to the East, that the tides of war would turn irrevocably. In 1942, the German army on the Eastern Front was weakened but still very powerful. In the north, the Wehrmacht continued the grim seige of Leningrad. Hundreds of thousands of Russian civilians had already died from starvation and shelling. In some places, corpses were stacked high in the streets.

> *"In summer, we picked up grass, boiled it, and ate it. It was food on our minds all the time ... All the days became one long day and night. Imagine nine hundred such days."*

The Germans facing Moscow clung to the defensive. But in the south, Hitler hungered for the coal of the Don Basin and the oil of the Caucasus. The key to defending the area was a sprawling industrial city on the Volga, a place that happened to be named after his arch-rival, **Stalingrad**.

To support the Wehrmacht were 20 divisions of weak Rumanian, Hungarian, Italian, and Spanish troops. Under Hitler's orders, Axis forces split up. One group boldly pushed far south to the River Don and beyond, driving nearly 400 miles into the mountainous Caucasus. By August 21, the Germans were closing in on the strategic oilwells at Baku—a goal they would never achieve.

The other group, the mighty Sixth Army under **General Friedrich von Paulus**, soon reached the Volga. Artillery and the Luftwaffe pounded Stalingrad round the clock. But the Russian soldiers and civilians defending the city converted the demolished buildings into a gigantic tank trap. And blindly, an arrogant Adolf Hitler ordered the Panzers into the rubble.

On September 13, the Nazis forced their way into the very heart of Stalingrad. The Soviets put up a desperate resistance, fighting block by block, house by house. Russian snipers were at every window, every doorway, every gap in a shattered wall. Panzers were all but useless in this wilderness of brick and stone:

"The street is no longer measured by meters, but in corpses ...
Stalingrad is no longer a town.
By day it is an enormous cloud of burning, blinding smoke; it is a vast furnace..."

By October 14, the Nazis controlled the south and center of the city. Now they launched an all-out attack at the tractor works in the north. Into this inferno, the Soviets fed only as many reinforcements as was absolutely necessary to continue the stuggle.

Just across the Volga, Marshal Zhukov was preparing a massive counter-attack. On the morning of November 19, 1942, the Red Army struck with the force of a million men. The main attack fell on the Rumanians, who guarded the northern flank of the river. The axis lines quickly collapsed —leaving nearly 30,000 Germans trapped in what Nazi propaganda would soon call **Fortress Stalingrad**.

Goering told Hitler there was nothing to worry about. The Luftwaffe, he swore, could easily supply von Paulus with the 600 tons of supplies needed each day. But bad weather kept many planes on the ground. And the Germans in Stalingrad began to starve. The General Staff urged Hitler to order the Sixth Army to fight its way out of the trap. Instead, he ordered a column of Panzers to break into the city. The Soviets stopped them 35 miles away, making escape impossible. An entire German Army was trapped in a hell of fire and ice.

"Around me everything is collapsing, a whole army is dying. Day and night are on fire..."

"I was shocked when I saw the map. We were entirely alone. Hitler had left us in the lurch ... So this is what the end looks like."

The Germans endured through the storms of November and snows of December. On January 10, von Paulus refused a Soviet surrender ultimatum. By January 24, both German airfields were captured. The men of the Sixth Army were now totally cut off.

On January 31, 1943, an emaciated Field Marshal von Paulus finally emerged from his frozen dugout and surrendered — together with the remaining 91,000 soldiers under his command. A Red Army man remembered the scene:

> *"For many days, columns and columns of German prisoners were passing by. The length of the columns was many, many kilometers long. They seemed never to end."*

The Russians now went on the attack and quickly broke through the thinned enemy lines. Through speed and discipline, most of the German troops were able to escape from the Caucasus before they were swept away by the overwhelming Soviet tide.

Within the Reich, somber drum rolls preceded the radio announcement of the crashing fall of **Fortress Stalingrad**. Four days of public mourning were declared. And Goebbels now began to stress the battle for national survival — not victory.

Adolf Hitler was never the same. The Russian Front became an obsession for him. He talked incessantly about the military situation all day. He labored over detailed maps through the night. He slept only with the aid of drugs.

For the rest of the war, the master of public speaking only twice again appeared in public. One of his last speeches was pre-recorded at his bunker, the *Wolf's Lair*, deep in the gloomy forests of East Prussia — surrounded by barbed wire and heavily armed SS troops, hundreds of miles from the capital in Berlin. And nearly a thousand miles from the graves at Stalingrad.

Chapter IX
CONQUEST OF THE PACIFIC

The American aircraft carriers and submarines spared at Pearl Harbor now came back to haunt Japan. In the Spring of 1942, **Colonel James Doolittle** convinced President Roosevelt to use a flattop to launch bombers on a daring attack.

On April 18, twelve specially modified B-25s took off from the carrier *USS Hornet*, 670 miles away from Japan. Each dropped a ton of bombs on Tokyo and quickly flew off in the direction of friendly airbases in China. Damage from the raid was minimal. Yet after the loss of Bataan, America was thrilled to finally land a blow at the enemy.

US submarines struck next. The men of the *silent service* were soon sinking more Imperial ships than all other American naval and air units combined. They would eventually cut the fragile lifeline of oil tankers and transports connecting the vast Japanese Empire.

Yet for the moment, Tokyo was still on the attack. Early in 1942, the Imperial Army sprang from its victory in Malaya and Singapore into neighboring Burma. The British were driven back hundreds of jungle miles to the Indian border, where they rallied and held. But the Japanese conquest of Burma cut the vital overland supply lines to another important ally: **China**.

Generalissimo Chiang Ki-Shek was the ruler of 500 million Chinese — who had long been at war with Japan. Chiang's Nationalist *Kuomintang* Army numbered millions, but it was poorly armed, fed, and trained. Worse, Chiang was also fighting a civil war in the west with Communists under the command of **Mao Zedung**.

Washington knew that holding China occupied nearly a million Japanese. It was essential to keep Chiang in the war, even if it meant supplying his army by air. To do this, transport aircraft based in India had to fly **The Hump** – the 20,000 foot high Himalaya mountain range. Over three years, a thousand US airman died accomplishing this goal. And somehow China survived.

In May of 1942, Japan began closing in on Australia, the last remaining allied bastion in the South Pacific. A mighty Imperial invasion fleet steamed toward Port Moresby on nearby New Guinea. US carriers *Yorktown* and *Lexington* rushed to intercept them.

The Battle of the Coral Sea was the first sea battle in history where opposing armies fought at a great distance with warplanes. As if blindfolded, Americans and Japanese sailed through dense fog and clouds. Then, on May 7, reconnaissance aircraft made contact.

Bombers and torpedo planes were launched. When the fighting stopped, each side had lost a flattop: the US *Lexington* and the Japanese *Shoho*. *Yorktown* was badly damaged and had to be sent to Hawaii for repairs. But the enemy was turned back.

Admiral Yamamoto now designed a trap to destroy the remaining US carriers. An Imperial fleet would pretend to attack the Aleutian islands off the coast of Alaska. But the real blow would fall on the small, strategic US airbase on the island of **Midway**.

Yamamoto's main invasion force had eight fast carriers and eleven battleships. He counted on quickly seizing Midway before enemy carriers could arrive. Then he would smash from the air any US flattops sent to the island's rescue. America would be driven out of the war once and for all.

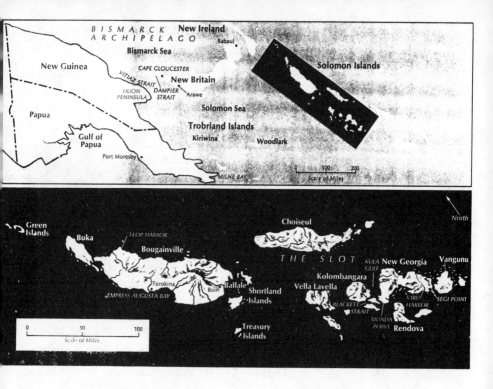

But what he didn't know was that Washington had cracked the Japanese code and was preparing a trap of its own. On June 3, US carriers *Enterprise* and *Hornet* secretly slipped into position near Midway. The third flattop to join the group, *Yorktown*, had been repaired in a record four days' time. American Admiral Chester Nimitz shrewdly anchored his fleet north of the island, just out of range of Japanese reconnaissance planes.

On the morning of June 4, Admiral Chuichi Nagumo, Japanese carrier commander, attacked Midway. The first wave of Imperial warplanes returned and was just being loaded with bombs for a second strike—when reconnaissance reported US flattops in the area. Nagumo frantically ordered his aircraft rearmed with torpedoes.

It was during this delay that that the first slow moving US torpedo planes arrived — and were promptly shot out of the sky. But a few moments later, wave after wave of lethal American divebombers suddenly appeared out of the clouds.

> *"The terrifying scream of the dive bombers reached me first, followed by the crashing explosion of a direct hit... Planes stood tail up, belching livid flame and jet-black smoke. Reluctant tears streamed down my cheeks as I watched the fires spread."*

Imperial carriers *Soryu*, *Kaga*, and *Akagi* were soon on fire and sinking. With the destruction of a fourth Japanese flattop the following day, Yamamoto ordered what was left of his fleet to safety. Only one US carrier, *USS Yorktown*, was lost. Here at Midway the Rising Sun first began to set.

From **Guadalcanal** now came another Japanese threat. Imperial forces were working furiously to complete an airfield on the small island that could threaten Australia. On August 7, 1942, exactly eight months after Pearl Harbor, America launched its first invasion of the war.

The reconquest of the Pacific began with just over 10,000 Marines coming ashore. They faced little opposition at first, and easily seized the enemy airfield and tons of supplies. But the Imperial Navy surprised the American fleet and destroyed four Allied cruisers. The US ships were driven far from Guadalcanal. And the Marines were left behind, on their own. This was the start of the bloody eight-month struggle for Guadalcanal.

It was also America's grim introduction to the realities of jungle fighting: heavy tropical rains, the overpowering stench of rotting vegetation and decomposing bodies, tall *kunai* grass that cut like a hacksaw, and clouds of fever causing mosquitoes. Soon the jungle heat and poor rations began to take their toll on both armies:

"The toughest part is going on, existing as an animal. Wet, cold, and hungry many times... Our stomachs have been ravaged with the food we've eaten and the way in which we eat. We've fought the Japs for water and cigarettes."

"We are nothing but skin and bones... I have become like a primitive man."

It took another six terrible months of battle to drive Imperial forces from Guadacanal.

Washington now proposed a two-pronged strategy for winning the war. MacArthur would start at Guadacanal, and use Allied ground and air forces to clear the enemy out of New Guinea and the islands in the South West Pacific. Meanwhile, the US Navy and Marines would make amphibious landings on key islands in the Central Pacific. These two mighty forces were scheduled to meet in the Philippines. There they'd unite for the final drive against Japan.

The Americans planned to use mobility, speed and surprise to "leap frog" over enemy strongpoints – leaving them isolated, out of the war. General MacArthur defined the new strategy like this:

"Hit 'em where they ain't."

SEABEES

The **Solomon Islands** were next. On November 1, US Marines leapfrogged to Bougainville, landing on a weakly-defended corner of the island. At first, there were few casualties. The Navy's **C**onstuction **B**attalion – known as the Fighting **Seabeas** – went to work carving an airstrip out of jungle.

The commander of the 40,000 Imperial troops hidden on the island rallied his men. The Japanese attacked in strength, and bitter fighting went on until the end of April 1944. Even before the Marines totally secured the island, US planes were already using the airfield to launch attacks on the powerful Japanese base on nearby Rabaul.

The war now shifted to the Central Pacific. Here America had to learn a different kind of fighting. The islands of the Gilbert chain were bare, rocky coral *atolls*. On November 20, a powerful US armada of six carriers and battleships assembed off the coast of **Tarawa** -- an island roughly the size of New York's Central Park. An American sailor viewing the intense bombardment wondered why "the whole goddamn island doesn't fall apart and sink."

Before the smoke cleared, the Marines began to come ashore in their new *amphtrack* amphibious tractor landing vehicles. But the island was ringed with a coral reef that the Japanese strengthened with treacherous four foot high coconut log sea wall, all in clear view of hidden guns dug into rock. The landing quickly became a massacre.

"They were knocking boats out left and right. A tractor'd get hit, stop, and burst into flame, with men jumping out like torches."

One out of four Americans storming Bloody Tarawa was killed or wounded. During the battle, the Japanese had to be blasted out of their underground blockhouses with high explosive and flame throwers. Once again, the Imperial troops simplified conquest by launching suicidal frontal attacks.

The hard lessons learned at Tarawa would reduce losses in invasions to come. Naval bombardments would go on much longer from now on. The *amphtracks* that brought the men ashore were also improved. These changes greatly reduced the costs of conquering **Kwajalein** and **Eniwetok,** in the neighboring Marshall Islands.

In June of 1944, America leapfrogged nearly a thousand miles to the **Marianas.** This strategic island chain was just within bombing range of Japan. A US Armada numbering 500 warships and 130,000 fighting men steamed into the Philippine Sea.

On June 15, the first Marines waded ashore on **Saipan**, a well-developed tropical island just 14 miles long. That night Japanese troops struck back. They were finally stopped dead at the beachhead by withering American fire.

Far out to sea, Japan was preparing an even more powerful counterpunch. Vice Admiral Jisaburo Ozawa had assembled practically every ship in the Imperial Navy – including nine carriers with 430 warplanes. He planned on using this force, together with 100 land-based aircraft on the Japanese held island of **Guam**, to smash the Americans in a giant pincer movement.

What Ozawa didn't know was that US subs had spotted the approach of his fleet. American warplanes struck first against Guam, severing one arm of the enemy pincer. On June 19, the Japanese launched their attack. Allied radar picked up approaching enemy planes from 150 miles away. And soon the air was filled with American fliers.

This great air battle is now called **The Marianas Turkey Shoot.** The Japanese pilots were young, inexperienced, and shortages of aviation fuel had limited their training. Within a matter of hours, Yanks downed 300 Imperial planes at a cost of only 30. Tokyo suffered even more losses when American subs sank an additional two Imperial carriers. Next day, US aircraft destroyed a third enemy flattop as it tried to slip away to safety.

Throughout the Pacific, the soldiers of the Rising Sun were now all alone. The nearby island of **Tinian** was seized by surprise. Heavy bombardment and a fake landing in the south caught the Japanese off guard. By nightfall, nearly 15,000 Marines came ashore. US tanks and infantry crushed the inevitable counterattack, conquering the island within a week.

Saipan and **Guam** were far tougher nuts to crack. By July 6, the Japanese had been pushed back into a small pocket on the top third of Saipan. Their commander, General Yoshitsugo Saito, realized that his situation was hopeless.

"We must utilize this opportunity to exalt true Japanese manhood. I will advance with those who remain to deliver yet another blow to the American Devils and leave my bones on Saipan as a bulwark of the Pacific."

The remaining 4,000 Imperial troops filled with *shiki* – the willingness to die in combat – now prepared to storm the lethal American wall of artillery fire and machine guns. Many were forced to climb over piles of their own dead to get to the Yanks.

The same horrific scenes were repeated on **Guam**, a rugged chunk of limestone 30 miles long. On July 20, Marines stormed ashore in the face of heavy enemy fire from caves and cliffs above the beach. After five terrible days of fighting, the Japanese were sealed off on a swampy peninsula. That night they attacked, many drunk with *sake*, shouting "Long live the Emperor. **Banzaii!**"

"An orange signal flare shot up from the Japanese lines. A singsong voice shouted into the night, and an avalanche of screaming forms bounded suddenly into view. With their bayonets gleaming in the light of sudden flares, they charged toward the Marine foxholes, throwing grenades and howling: Ban-zai-ai!"

On **Saipan**, hundreds of Japanese civilians killed themselves rather than surrender. Battle-hardened US Marines watched in shock as parents threw their children off high cliffs and leaped after them. Other Japanese waded out into the ocean to drown. One group unfurled the Imperial flag and the detonated grenades against their chests. The orgy of self-destruction went on until all were dead.

The fall of the Marianas meant that long range US bombers based there could strike the Japanese home islands for the first time since Doolittle's raid. Perhaps this is why Emperor Hirohito was heard to say: *"Now hell is on us."*

CHAPTER TEN: SMASHING THE AXIS

As Rommel warned, North Africa was a giant trap. From east and west, Allied Armies closed in on the Axis stronghold of Tunisia. In February of 1943, Germans fought with their backs to the sea — which the British now controlled. Supplies were soon cut off.

The Americans were still green, inexperienced at war. As they rolled from the western desert into the **Kasserine Pass**, the Germans panzers struck. GIs panicked and were quickly overrun. Nearly 2,400 were captured, along with great stores of equipment.

Yet nothing could change the fact that the weary Afrika Korps was stretched to the breaking point. As Monty and the Americans closed in, the Germans frantically shifted from one side of Tunisia to the other. On May 7, they finally cracked.

Tunis fell to the British a week later. For most of the 150,000 Axis troops abandoned in Tunisia, there was no escape. Hitler's two-year African adventure had come to an end.

Now it was Europe's turn. Stalin demanded a **Second Front** in the West to draw off German strength from Russia. The Allies targeted Italy – the weakest link in the Axis.

On July 9, 1943, nearly 100,000 Allied troops began landing on the south coast of the large island of **Sicily**. Most of Italian troops surrendered, but the Germans fought back. In the East, Monty's troops liberated Syracuse but got bogged down in the mountains. In the West, Patton had more ground to cover, but he threw caution to the wind.

On July 20, US tanks reached Palermo. Italians showered the liberators with flowers. The Wehrmacht fought its way back to the port of Messina, where 60,000 Germans managed to escape to Italy. On August 17, Sicily fell.

Mussolini's fortunes had already fallen. On July 24, he had summoned the Fascist Grand Council to raise sagging morale. Instead, the Fascisti ordered *Il Duce* to yield control of the Army and the State to King Victor Emmanuel. All Italy exploded with joy.

The next day, Mussolini was arrested, taken away in an ambulance, and imprisoned. Hitler now played a waiting game. As long as Italy stayed in the Axis, Germany would make no move.

On September 3, Monty's Eighth Army crossed over from Sicily and advanced rapidly up the eastern side of the Italian boot. Fascist leader Marshal Pietro Badoglio, began frantically negotiating with the Allies. Five days later, Radio Roma announced a ceasefire. Within a month, Italy declared war on Germany.

But first it was Hitler's turn. The Wehrmacht disarmed hundreds of thousands of Italian troops. Rome and other key cities were quickly occupied.

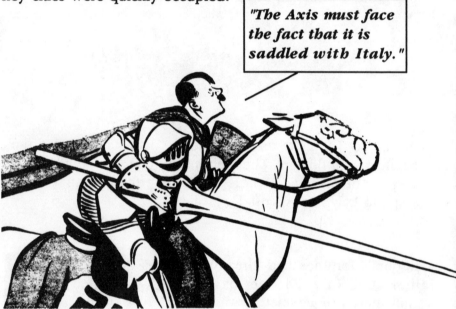

"The Axis must face the fact that it is saddled with Italy."

The Fuehrer now ordered the daring rescue of Mussolini. An elite SS commando unit used gliders to raid the mountain resort where *Il Duce* was kept captive. He was then flown to Germany and put at the head of a puppet Fascist regime in the north of Italy. But the once-swaggering dictator was a broken man.

On September 9, US amphibious forces began landing at **Salerno**—south of the strategic Bay of Naples. German guns and tanks pounded the beaches, threatening to push the GIs back into the sea. American cooks, truckers, and mechanics were rushed in to hold the line. Massive air strikes eventually forced the Germans to withdraw.

The Germans abandoned Naples on October 1, after destroying the port area. Allied troops moving into the city received an ecstatic welcome from its people. Yet the enemy still barred the Allied approach to Rome – just 100 miles away.

Italy was perfect for defence: narrow, crisscrossed by mountain ranges and swift rivers. German commander, **Field Marshal Albert Kesselring,** exploited terrain and unusually bad weather to slow the Allied advance.

The American troops were fighting knee-deep in mud. Thousands of men had not been dry for weeks. Other thousands lay at night in the high mountains with the temperature below freezing and thin snow sifting over them. For tens of thousands, it was like living in prehistoric times.

On January 22, 1944, Americans landed north of the enemy at the resort of **Anzio** – only 33 miles from Rome. The roads into the Eternal City were wide open. Yet the US commander on the beachhead paused too long to build up strength. And Kesselring threw a murderous wall of steel around the invaders.

For months, the GIs lived under constant shelling in the rubble of Anzio. It took the destruction of the medieval abbey on *Monte Cassino* – a German stronghold – before Kesselring pulled back to his next line of defenses. Rome still remained in German hands.

In Russia, Hitler demanded yet another glorious Blitzkrieg. It seemed an easy task to pinch off the bulge in the Soviet lines around the city of **Kursk**, and bag a half million prisoners. Yet once again, the Fuehrer refused to face facts. Most German divisions were only at half strength after the losses at Stalingrad. Tanks and aircraft had to be stripped from the Western and Southern fronts to fill the gaps.

"Leave me. I am relying on my intuition."

Soviet intelligence had learned of Hitler's plan. Within months, the Russians dug hundreds of miles of minefields around Kursk. They moved in 20,000 heavy guns, and over a thousand *Katyusha* rocket launchers. And then the waited for the Nazis to blunder into the trap.

On July 5, the Germans attacked in a pincer movement. Heavily armed Tiger tanks pushed north and south—but even they could not completely break through the 50-mile deep Soviet defenses. After a week of futile assaults, the German attack ground to a halt.

Now the Red Army struck. Its tanks and lend-lease American trucks gave the Soviets new mobility. In a single week, they drove the weakened Wehrmacht back over 100 miles, cutting off whole divisions. The Germans panicked, ran, and died by the tens of thousands.

The Soviet steamroller kept rolling westward. Kharkov was liberated on August 23, followed by Orel and Belograd. In November, Germans were driven out of the Ukrainian capital of Kiev. By January 1944, two-thirds of occupied Soviet territory had been recovered.

БУДЕТ СВОБОДНОЙ!

Hitler now had to fight yet another battle—in the skies above Germany. In May of 1942, Churchill sent 1,000 bombers to devastate Cologne. They obliterated it in a single night. At this stage in the war, cities seemed to be the only thing the RAF could hit with any effect.

In August 1942, *Flying Fortresses* of the US Eighth Air Force began flying missions out of Britain. Planners hoped that heavily armed groups of B-17s could fly above enemy aircraft *flak* and fight off the Luftwaffe—while conducting daytime pinpoint bombing of strategic oil refineries and factories. They soon discovered their error.

"You can't imagine how it feels to be flying at 20,000 feet with your oxygen mask on, with the temperature down to 30 degrees below zero. Ahead of you lies the target and flak ... hundreds and hundreds of black puffs, just like a cloud – all you can do is sit there and sweat, knowing you've got to ride right into it."

US Airmen were now met by accurate radar-controlled ground fire and a swift new enemy fighter – the *Focke-Wulf 190*. In just one strategic strike over Germany in October 1943, 60 out of 300 B-17s were lost.

German cities remained highly vulnerable—especially after dark. In late July and August of 1943, RAF Lancaster heavy bombers staged night attacks on the port of Hamburg. The attack caused a gigantic firestorm—*Die Katastrophe*—which killed an estimated 43,000, and made a million more homeless. Even those who reached bomb shelters were no longer safe, as the firestorm asphyxiated its victims.

> *"We tried to get out, but we couldn't. The building over us was hit by an incendiary bomb and was on fire. The outside walls had collapsed ... We were half suffocated. We couldn't breathe ..."*

Yet even the death of so many German civilians failed to slow war production. Hitler's architect, **Albert Speer**, performed miracles with industry. Factories were decentralized, camouflaged, or hidden deep underground. In short time, German war production actually began to rise. And so did Allied air losses.

For precision bombing to work, the Allies needed a long-range fighter to challenge the Luftwaffe on its own turf. In December of 1943, they found it: the **P-51 Mustang**. Fast, manueverable, and heavily armed, the fighter was called "Little Friend" by grateful bombardiers. With this new weapon, came a bold new strategy.

Early in 1944, America took the war to the Luftwaffe. The US plan was to target and destroy Germany's planes and pilots, its factories and installations. This would smash the Reich's ability to resist strategic bombing. And it would clear the way for the coming Allied invasion of Europe.

Big Week began on February 20, 1944 as thousands of Allied bombers pounded Germany day and night. Losses were heavy, but 450 German fighters were knocked out. In desperation, the Luftwaffe tried to avoid combat. So the Allies switched the attack to Berlin and other cities. The Luftwaffe had to rise to this challenge. The result was an epic dogfight.

Goering suffered losses he could no longer afford. Allied bombers now targeted enemy oil facilities. Starting in April, US B-24 *Liberator* bombers operating out of Italy bombed the massive Rumanian petrol installations at Ploesti. A month later, Germany's synthetic oil facilities were smashed. The Reich had lost 90% of its fuel production.

The war *underground* began heating up everywhere. Anti-Nazi rebellion soon spread through Europe. For the brave men and women of the **Resistance**, the price of capture or betrayal was torture and a cruel death. Yet the drone of Allied planes overhead — as well as news of Alamein, Stalingrad, and the fall of Italy — encouraged millions.

In the East, Soviet partisans aided the advance of the Red Army by destroying German trains and communications. In Yugoslavia, **Marshall Tito** led the world's most effective guerrilla army. Communist partisans in this mountainous land tied down an estimated 15 German divisions. And in Poland, patriots readied arms for a massive uprising.

Even in totalitarian Germany itself, small resistance groups began to spread. One brave cell of students and veterans called themselves the **White Rose**. They defied the terror of the Gestapo to distribute anti-Nazi leaflets. In 1943, the leaders were captured and executed, leaving this warning:

> *"The day of reckoning has come, the day when German youth will settle accounts with the vilest tyranny ever endured by our nation."*

In the West, the people of Denmark used civil disobedience and strikes to protest German occupation. When Jews were ordered to wear the hated Yellow Stars, the Danish King appeared wearing a Yellow Star of his own. Danish Resistance members bravely smuggled most of the nation's 5,000 Jews to safety in neutral Sweden.

In France, the Resistance had two battles to fight. The first was against the Germans. And the second was against fellow countrymen collaborating with the Nazis. To their shame, French police had participated in the roundup and deportation of Jews to Germany. And heavily armed thugs from the fascist paramilitary group known as the *Milice* – the Militia – were doing the German's dirty work, spreading terror, and battling Resistance fighters.

Anti-Nazi men and women risked their lives to save hundreds of downed Allied aviators. They printed numerous underground newspapers, organized sabotage, and formed armed fighting units called the *Maquis* out in the open country. Nearly every town had its martyrs. The Resistance would soon play an even greater role in the coming battle for the liberation of Europe.

Chapter XI
THE FALL OF FORTRESS EUROPA

In Spring of 1944, the largest invasion force in history was ready to liberate Hitler's Fortress Europa. A million and a half American troops and another million British and Canadian had massed in England under command of General Dwight Eisenhower.

Nearly 8,000 airplanes and five million tons of invasion supplies had been stockpiled: mountains of ammunition, fuel, chewing gum and even plywood coffins. Whole towns, vast sections of this very traditional society had to be evacuated to make way for the build-up. Many Britons found the lively GIs a touch of excitement in weary old England. But others complained that the Yanks were:

> *"Overpaid, oversexed, and over here."*

The coming invasion was codenamed **Operation Overlord**. All had been carefully timed to tides and moon. But storms threatened. Rather than postpone the invasion for a month, Eisenhower took the biggest gamble of his life. He okayed *D-Day* for June 6, 1944. Before dawn, three divisions of Allied airborne and glider troops were dropped east and west of the beachead.

British troops quickly captured the bridges linking a powerful Panzer division to the beaches. But US airborne and glider forces were dumped all over Normandy. Confusion reigned on both sides of the battle.

Germany's **Atlantic Wall** was commanded by the youngest Field Marshal in the Wehrmacht, Edwin Rommel. The old Desert Fox had overseen the creation of a coastal defence system of forts and bunkers, supported by four million explosive mines.

159

But Rommel was away in Germany when the landings began. It was Field Marshal von Rundstedt who first heard reports of Allied activity. As a precaution, he mobilized his Panzers. But Headquarters in Berlin cancelled this order — which required the Fuehrer's personal permission. And the Fuehrer was fast asleep.

Under cover of darkness and fog, over 5,000 Allied invasion ships now approached the coast of France. The big guns aboard the Allied warships opened fire. At 6:30 sharp, GIs started coming ashore at **Utah** and **Omaha** beaches.

At Utah, intense naval bombardment shattered German defenses. US amphibious tanks rose out the waves and onto the sand, right into the midst of the stunned enemy. But Bloody Omaha was a disaster. Amphibious tanks sank in choppy seas. Landing craft let down their ramps too soon, spilling some men out into six feet of rough water. Others were perfect targets for the German machine guns.

"It was a weird experience. Young men cryin' for their mothers, wetting and defecating themselves. Others telling jokes. Most of us were just solemn."

"The water was cold and the beach still more than a hundred yards away. The bullets tore holes in the water around me, and I made for the nearest steel obstacle."

Dug into the cliffs was a network of fortified German guns. There were only two exits out of this killing ground – both of them heavily mined. For the men who managed to reach the beaches, there was no place to go. Hundreds of dead and dozens of wrecked vehicles littered the shore. After many hours of punishment, an American officer rallied his men with these tough words:

"Two kinds of people are staying on this beach, the dead and those who are going to die – now let's get the hell out of here."

Further to the east, troops from England and Canada landed on **Gold, Juno,** and **Sword** beaches. It was exactly four years and a day since Dunkirk. These tough, experienced soldiers swept ashore with special tanks equipped with flame throwers, mine destroying devices, and heavy guns for smashing enemy bunkers. Within hours, they'd pushed beyond the beaches and linked up. A vast army behind them was already coming ashore from hundreds of landing craft and portable docks.

Hitler was in pajamas when he learned about Normandy. He feared that the invasion might just be a diversion for more serious landings at Calais – a port closer to England. By the time he ordered the Panzers to roll, it was too late.

"Spurts of fire flicked along the column and splashes of dust staccatoed the road. Everyone was piling out of the vehicles and scuttling for the neighboring fields. Several vehicles were already in flames."

Swift and deadly, hundreds of Allied fighter bombers smashed the Panzers from above. Germans were now forced to move at night, and only on backroads. Railways throughout France had been destroyed by bombing and the determined French Resistance – which committed 900 acts of sabotage on D-Day alone. At the headquarters of Field Marshal von Rundstedt, the mood was grim.

"End the war! What else can you do?"

What Hitler did was remove Rundstedt and unleash secret **V**engeance weapons. Not on the landing zones. But once again on the British people. To convert them, he said, to peace.

The **V-1**s were pilotless jets loaded with explosives.

Despite the punishment, the spirit of Britain refused to break. But Germany's spirit was already cracking.

On July 20, Colonel Klaus von Stauffenberg smuggled a briefcase filled with explosives into Hitler's East Prussian headquarters. Stauffenberg was an injured war hero, and part of a group of Army leaders who planned an uprising against the Nazis. When the bomb went off, four died. The Fuehrer was wounded in the arm and suffered burns. His nerves were shaken by the blast, but not his urge for revenge:

"I will crush and destroy the criminals who have dared oppose themselves to Providence and me."

The plot immediately fell apart when word of Hitler's survival reached Berlin. The Gestapo arrested 15,000 suspects. Some, like Stauffenberg, were shot on the spot. Others conspirators, like Field Marshal Rommel, were offered a chance to save their family by swallowing poison. Many were slowly strangled from meathooks in Nazi prisons. A movie of their final agony was specially made on Hitler's orders.

Yet Nazi terror was no substitute for victory. A million Anglo-American troops were crammed into Normandy by June 27, the day the city of Cherbourg fell. But rough terrain and tough German resistance slowed the Allied advance.

On July 18, GIs smashed their way into the town of St. Lô. Armored units under General Patton now rolled north to link up with the British. Nearly 100,000 Germans were captured as the Wehrmacht tried to flee to the Rhine. The road to Paris was open.

> *"Every Frenchman seems to feel it is his duty*
> *to shake hands with every American he sees..."*

On August 15, more Allied troops landed in the south of France. These soldiers joined 50,000 Resistance fighters to clear the southern half of the country.

On August 19, Paris erupted in rebellion. Hitler ordered the German commandant, General Dietrich von Choltitz, to torch the city. Instead, Choltitz opened hasty negotiations with the Allies. French armored forces entered the capital on August 25, 1944, followed by a full American division. The next day, a triumphant General Charles de Gaulle marched past cheering millions.

"There are moments which surpass every one of our poor lives."

In Eastern Europe, Soviet troops and partisans now launched a great offensive. Again, Hitler foolishly ordered his men to stand and die. The Wehrmacht lost a million dead, wounded, or captured. On July 18, the Russian steamroller crossed into German East Prussia. Morale was high. So was the desire for revenge.

"Today there are no books; today there are no stars in the sky; today there is only one thought: Kill the Germans."

In August, the non-Communist Polish Home Army rose in revolt. Stalin chose this very moment to halt the Soviet tanks just across the river from Warsaw. For the next three months, the Poles fought an uneven battle in the streets of the doomed city. Nearly 200,000 died.

"We are waiting for thee, red pest,
To deliver us from black death."

In the West, supply lines to the front now stretched hundreds of miles. Hopes for a quick leap into Germany were dashed when a bold Allied airborne attack on the Rhine bridge at **Remagen** was crushed by heavy Panzer counterattack.

165

The Fuehrer now approved a final Blitzkrieg which we today call the **Battle of the Bulge**. Once again, the blow fell in the *impassable* Ardennes Forest. Nazi commandos in GI uniform seized crossroads and bridges, spreading confusion. Then 28 German divisions emerged out of the woods to surprise four American divisions, many of them green recruits. Bad weather kept Allied airpower out of the skies, allowing the Panzers to cut a large bulge in the Allied lines. Thousand of Yanks were cut off and captured, but most fought back.

The GIs fell back to **Bastogne**, an important road juncture. Just before Panzers encircled the town, the veteran US 101st Airborne Division managed to slip inside. These rugged paratroopers helped man the icy foxholes in the desperate days to come. When the Germans offered surrender, the reply was short and defiant: *"Nuts."*

Just before Christmas, 1944, the weather cleared enough for US planes to drop supplies. Patton's tanks now battled their way into Bastogne, lifting the siege. The attack had failed. Germany lost 120,000 troops. Panzers and trucks had to be abandoned for lack of fuel. When Hitler finally ordered a withdrawal in January of 1945, the once mighty Wehrmacht limped home on foot.

On February 4, Stalin, Churchill, and an ailing Roosevelt met in the Russian city of **Yalta** to hammer out postwar policy. The Big Three made plans for dividing Germany into occupation zones. Stalin even agreed to allow free elections in the newly liberated nations of Eastern Europe. But secretly he had other plans:

> *"Whoever occupies a territory imposes his own social system. Everyone imposes his system as far as his army can advance."*

Two days after Yalta, 1200 US and British heavy bombers staged a controversial attack on Dresden. Critics claim the bombing of this historic German city was to demonstrate Anglo-American airpower to Stalin. Over l00,000 perished in the firestorm that swept the city. The "fantastic glow" of the flames could be seen from the air 200 miles away. Goebbels tried to get his people to see the bright side of things:

"The fewer cities there are left in Germany, the more we will be free to fight."

Early in March 1945, American tanks finally crossed over the Rhine into Germany. Patton's tanks were only 50 miles from Berlin when Ike ordered a halt on the line agreed upon at Yalta. On this same day, April 12, President Roosevelt died of a cerebral hemorrhage in Washington, DC. People mourned throughout the world.

Deep in their bunker, Hitler and Goebbels imagined that their luck had changed. Yet Vienna fell to the Red Army the next day. On April 25, Americans and Soviets met at the town of Torgau, on the river Elbe. It was a rare moment in world history:

"We drank and there were accordions and balalaikas and music and dancing. They played American songs... Russian girls dancing. It was a strange sight."

Stunned Allied troops now liberated the last of Hitler's Death Camps. Ike turned pale. Old *Blood and Guts* Patton was so affected that he slipped behind a barracks to get sick. The smell of death was everywhere. Corpses were stacked like cordwood. Piles of human ashes and bones filled the cremetoria. Starving, sick, often in shock, the living lay helpless next to the dead:

"We went into the children's hut. The floors had been piled with corpses there had been no time to move."

"I didn't feel anything at all except Jesus Christ Jesus Christ Jesus Christ..."

"You can't understand it even when you've seen it."

On April 25, the Red Army encircled Berlin. Deep in his underground bunker, Hitler continued to shout orders and threaten, moving nonexistent divisions around the map. Aides remember him as a stooped figure with a pale and puffy face, hunched in his chair, hands trembling.

The Nazi regime was now down to its final days. Old men and boys were forced into the *Volksturm* – the people's storm brigades. While Himmler and Goering tried to escape, Hitler made plans to drag the whole nation down with him into total destruction.

The full horror of war now fell on the people of Berlin. With Soviet tanks only blocks away, panic spread. *SS* fanatics hunted down deserters and hanged them from the nearest pole. A weary German officer recorded the chaotic final hours of the Thousand Year Reich.

"The night is fiery red. Heavy shelling. Otherwise a terrible silence... Women and children huddling in niches and listening to the sound of battle... Nervous breakdowns."

On August 28, Italian partisans executed Mussolini and his mistress, hung them upside down, and left them to be spat upon by the people. Hitler knew his time had come.

On April 29, the Fuehrer married his longtime lover, Eva Braun. Then he dictated a political testament in which the Jews were again blamed for starting the war. On April 30, ten days after his fiftieth birthday, Adolf Hitler shot himself in the head. His body, and that of his new wife, were burned in a bomb crater above the bunker. Goebbels, his wife, and their six children poisoned themselves.

On May 8, 1945, Germany surrendered unconditionally. After six years of war, it was finally **V-E** Day, victory in Europe. The long nightmare was almost over.

Chapter Twelve:
BANGS & Whimpers

"People of the Philippines, I have returned."

The sun was quickly setting on the Japanese Empire. Hundreds of US warships — the greatest armada in history   now converged on the Philippines. On October 20, 1944, the long awaited invasion began with a landing on the island of Leyte.

Tokyo now scraped together its remaining naval power for a final attack. The **Battle of Leyte Gulf** began when a group of Imperial carriers, lacking warplanes, tried to lure the main US strike force north, away from the Philippines. Admiral "Bull" Halsey fell for the bait and chased after them with his own carriers, sinking four enemy flattops from the air.

With Halsey far away, two groups of Japanese battleships and cruisers steamed unopposed into Leyte Gulf. The southern force was spotted at the last minute and sailed right into the waiting guns of American warships. But the larger, central force blasted its way to the heart of the Allied invasion fleet.

Here 16 small US escort carriers were defended by a thin screen of lightly armed destroyers. In the confusion, three Imperial cruisers were sunk at the cost of an escort carrier and three destroyers. But the Japanese feared that Halsey's carrier force was returning, and broke off the attack before shelling the Americans on the beaches.

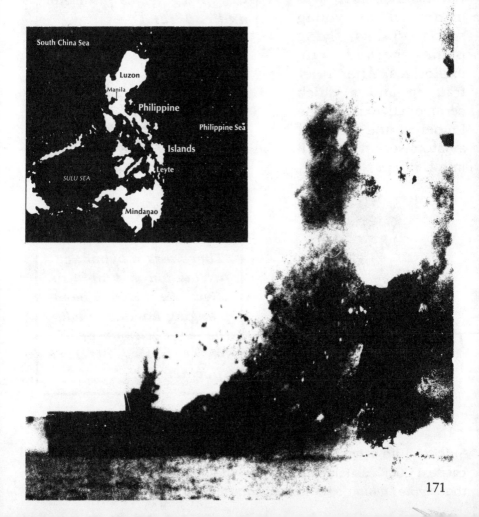

Tokyo now unveiled a desperate new weapon: **Kamikaze**. It was a word that referred to the **divine wind** which destroyed a Mongol invasion fleet long ago. But this *kamikaze* was made up of young suicide pilots flying planes packed with explosives. After brief training and a quick ceremonial toast to the Emperor, the doomed aviators set off to crash into US ships.

"Like cherry blossoms in the spring, let us fall clean and radiant."

"There was a hypnotic fascination in a sight so alien. We watched each plunging kamikaze with the detached horror of one witnessing a terrible spectacle."

Suicide pilots would eventually sink over 300 US ships and cause 15,000 casualties. Yet even the fanatical determination of the *divine wind* could not turn the tide in the Philippines.

During months of brutal jungle fighting on Leyte and neighboring Luzon, several hundred thousand Japanese were killed, captured, or scattered to the hills. On February 3, 1945, US troops finally battled their way into Manila. Nearly 5,000 Allied prisoners were freed from the hell of prison camps. Most were walking skeletons.

Iwo Jima was the next step. These eight square miles of black volcanic ash and rock, only 775 miles from Japan, would make the perfect airbase. US Marines landed on February 20, and quickly encountered some of the most bitter fighting of the war.

The Imperial Army had converted Iwo into a fortress of concrete pillboxes, tunnels, and minefields. Americans had to advance on their bellies inch by inch over a blasted terrain that soon resembled the landscape of the moon. Japanese artillery dug into **Mount Suribachi** dominated the battle until February 23, when Marines finally seized the peak.

We raised the Stars and Stripes over the real Japanese empire ... I was never so scared in my life before."

Bloody Iwo claimed the lives of nearly 7,000 brave Marines and 20,000 equally fearless Japanese. Only 212 Imperial troops surrendered. Yet within days, America had leap-frogged another 400 hundred miles closer to the enemy heartland – to **Okinawa**.

This large island was the ideal springboard for an all-out invasion of Japan. On April 1, Easter Sunday, US Marines hit the beaches unopposed. The Japanese had withdrawn inland to escape heavy bombardment. There was little contact until five days into the invasion. Then Japan struck. From the air.

Tokyo sent its last 1,000 planes against the powerful invasion fleet. In the first hours, six American warships were sunk by Kamikaze attack. The air assault continued for days, eventually taking the lives of 5,000 seamen.

"I leave for the attack with a smile on my face... The moon will be full tonight. As I fly over the open sea off Okinawa I will choose the enemy ship that is to be my target."

The slaughter then shifted to the land. The Yanks used flamethrowers and high explosives to clear out well-placed enemy bunkers. Tokyo's 100,000 troops fought on desperately. When Imperial defenses finally began to crack, the order was given for fierce *Banzai* attacks. Resistance totally ended on June 22, 1945. For the first time in the war, a large number of Japanese — 11,000 in all — surrendered.

Yet the diehard militarists in Tokyo would never give up. A member of the Imperial Cabinet compared the situation to a bicycle rolling down a hill without brakes. The Army, it was said, did not know how to surender.

A million soldiers were stuck in China. The fleet and the air force were gone. US subs had sunk most of the transports Japan needed to fuel and feed itself. Even rice had run out. Then, starting late in 1944, death arrived from the air.

Long range B-29 *Superfortresses* based in the Marianas began dropping new types of incendiary bombs filled with napalm — a lethal mix of magnesium and jellied gasoline. On March 9, 1945, heavy air attacks on Tokyo created a firestorm which swept through the wooden structures of the city, killing 100,000 in a single night.

"The fires were incredible now with flames leaping hundreds of feet into the air ... Wherever I turned my eyes, I saw people running away from the school grounds seeking air to breathe."

Osaka, Kobe, Nagoya were next. The US bombing campaign soon became the single greatest disaster in all of Japanese history. And now a new, even more terrible weapon was being readied for use...

The **Atomic Bomb**. Albert Einstein, Nobel Prize winning physicist and a Jewish refugee from Hitler's Germany, had warned President Roosevelt in 1938 that the Nazis might be the first to create a nuclear weapon. After Pearl Harbor, America accelerated its top secret atomic research. A crash program was funded — costing 2 billion wartime dollars — codenamed *The Manhattan Project*.

Dr. Robert Oppenheimer, a brilliant theoretical physicist, was put in charge of the project. After years of work at an isolated Army base at Los Alamos, New Mexico, history's first A-Bomb was placed high atop a tower at a deserted place known as Alamogordo. At exactly 5:30 a.m. on July 16, 1945, a nuclear chain reaction was produced. A scientist ten miles away compared the heat of the blast to opening a hot oven. The world would never be the same.

Oppenheimer and other scientists urged the White House to demonstrate the Bomb's power to Japan — before dropping it. The new President was former Vice President **Harry S. Truman.** The Manhattan Project had been so secret that Truman received his first briefing only after the death of FDR in April 1945.

President Truman saw the A-Bomb in military terms. He had been shocked by the ferocity of Japanese suicide attacks and hoped to force a quick end to the war. This would save the lives of an estimated million Americans who were expected to die invading Japan.

"Last night the whole weight of the moon and stars fell on me."

In Tokyo, the Army barred direct talks with the Alies. So Emperor Hirohito secretly ordered his civilian ministers to find a way to make peace. Messages were quietly sent to neutral countries that Japan wanted to come to terms. But time was running out for diplomacy.

In late July of 1945, the **Big Three** Allies met at Potsdam in defeated Germany. Truman and Churchill clashed with Stalin over the imposition of Communist rule in countries liberated by the Red Army. This event today is usually seen as the beginning of the Cold War between East and West. It was also here in Potsdam that the President first learned that the United States had a working Atom Bomb.

On July 26, the Allies announced **The Potsdam Declaration**. It demanded the total, unconditional surrender of Japan. It promised that the nation would not be enslaved or destroyed. But it demanded the removal from power of the militarists who started the war. And it warned that refusal meant *prompt and utter destruction*.

The Japanese Army still refused to consider peace unless the rule of the divine Emperor was guaranteed and any thought of Allied occupation dispelled. The Prime Minister publicly mocked the Declaration and again promised victory.

The final countdown now began. On the morning of August 6, 1945, a B-29 bomber called the *Enola Gay* took off from the island of Tinian. It carried a uranium bomb that measured 28 inches wide by 120 long, weighed 9,000 pounds, and packed the punch of twenty thousand tons of dynamite. Because of its relatively small size, it was called "Little Boy."

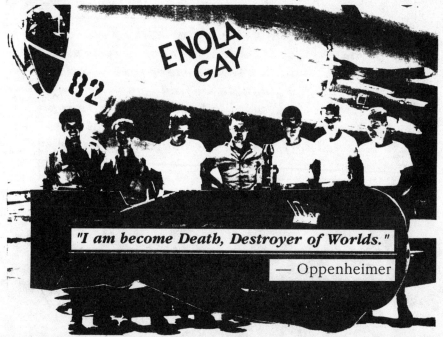

"I am become Death, Destroyer of Worlds."
— Oppenheimer

The Enola Gay reached Hiroshima around 8:15 a.m. Air raid sirens went off as workers rushed to their jobs and children hurried to school. Many paused to watch the lone bomber flying overhead. The Atomic Age began at exactly 8:15 and 17 seconds when "Little Boy" was released. A moment later, American Aviators wearing special glasses saw a purple flash far below them:

"My God, what have we done?"

"Then I saw a big flash in the sky, so I hid my face on the ground. I remember that I must have been blown away by the impact. I couldn't find any of my friends... All my clothes were torn away except my undergarments. My skin just peeled off and was hanging from my body."

The bomb exploded 2,000 feet above the center of the city, incinerating 60 percent of Hiroshima. Steel girders melted like wax. Railway trains were lifted hundreds of feet into the air. Trees and telephone poles exploded like matches. Human beings simply vaporized. A shock wave leveled houses miles away from Ground Zero — the point where the bomb exploded. **More than 70,000 died instantly**. Thousands more would later perish from burns and radiation sickness.

Yet the Imperial Army still refused to surrender. On August 9, a second atomic bomb filled with radioactive plutonium was dropped on the city of **Nagasaki**. Because of its swollen shape, this device was called "Fat Boy." The bomb missed the center of the city by three miles, but was still powerful enough to kill 40,000 people.

The next day, Hirohito told his cabinet that continuation of the war meant the death of Japan. Army fanatics now prepared for revolt. The Prime Minister's residence was machine gunned, and the homes of several members of the Cabinet were burned. Soldiers were even placed around the entrance of the Imperial Palace.

On August 15, Hirohito slipped free of house arrest. For the first time in history, the Emperor spoke to his people over the radio. Choosing his words carefully, he admitted that the war had not gone to Japan's advantage.

"We have decided to affect a settlement of the present situation by resorting to extraordinary measures."

Though fearing to use the word, he meant *surrender*. On this day, **V-J Day,** the world celebrated victory over Japan. The Imperial Army was ordered to lay down its guns. On five continents, millions poured into the streets to celebrate with ecstatic singing, hugging, and kissing. Church bells rang, music blared, fireworks lit the sky. After years of wartime blackouts, lights now blazed through the night.

On September 2, 1945, the Japanese signed the document of surrender aboard the US battleship *Missouri,* moored in Tokyo Harbor. US General MacArthur stayed on in Japan to govern. *The war was over!*

But what about peace? With Europe and Japan desolated, the power in the world now shifted to the US and USSR. The border between the two systems quickly hardened into what Churchill called an **Iron Curtain**. Eastern Europe fell under harsh Communist rule. The division of Germany became permanent.

One of the few things East and West could agree upon was bringing enemy war criminals to justice. In late 1945, top Nazi leaders were tried at an international court convened in Nuremberg, West Germany. America would later do the same in Japan.

While the world was stunned by evidence of the horrors practiced by the Third Reich – former Reichsmarschall Goering seemed almost bored. In the end, he cheated execution by suicide. But many other top Nazis went to the gallows. The **Nuremberg Trials** gave the world a new code of military conduct. No longer could a soldier be expected to carry out orders leading to crimes against humanity.

The **United Nations** was created in 1945 to settle world conflicts. Yet this peacekeeping role was limited by the right of the superpowers to veto actions of which they disapprove. Since that time, hundreds of small wars have erupted around the world, many supported by the US and USSR.

Ironically, it is the threat of war between the superpowers that has kept the peace. A single 100 megaton hydrogen (nuclear) bomb has more destructive power than all the weapons used in World War II. Thousands of nuclear weapons are in place today around the world. Trillions of dollars and rubles have been squandered buying this uncertain peace.

Yet World War II also brought positive changes. Throughout **Asia** and **Africa,** hundreds of millions of colonized people grew restless in their chains. They saw their European masters humbled. They had heard the Allies talk about fighting for freedom and the rights of man. Popular movements were rising up to challenge the old Empires. Soon dozens of independent new nations would join the world community.

Reacting to the Soviet threat, Western Europe was able to unite for the first time in a thousand years. The ideology of dictatorship and racism had been discredited. Everywhere science and technology made immense strides. Yet all of these advances must be weighed against the suffering of war.

In 1945, half the world was in ruins. Tens of millions were sick, starving, homeless. Cities were in ruins. Vast areas lacked basic services such as water, sanitation, medical care, or electricity. And what of the dead? Simply printing the names of the 40 million men, women, and children who perished during World War II would require a book thousands of times the size of this one. Yet in their memory, let the survivors have the last word.

"My father... he cannot be alone in closed room. After Gestapo. He must know he can open the door. He cannot travel in trains because the door is closed. Never again."

"When my children ask, "Tell us about the war," I can't tell them anything."

"Never again."

Errol Selkirk spent his boyhood fighting and refighting the major battles of World War II. It's taken three decades for peace to catch up with him. Now, when not writing *Beginners* books, he prefers to stay at home in bed. (See *Erotica for Beginners*.)

Naomi Rosenblatt - When she's not making trouble or whoopie, she's often making *Beginners* books. This is her sixth. When she wins Lotto, she hopes to make an artists' colony near a tropical rainforest in support of all endangered species, including artists. (See *Rainforests for Beginners*.)

Shey Wolvek-Pfister is a painter, mother and pacifist who lives in a Brooklyn brownstone with a man, a child, a cat and a rabbit. Longing for a yet more *nature*-al environment, she hopes to live in West Africa someday. (See *African History for Beginners*.)

FURTHER READING

The American Heritage Picture History of World War II, ed. C.L. Sulzberger. New York. 1966.

Before The Deluge: A Portrait of Berlin in the 1920s, Otto Friedrich. Fromm International Publishing Corporation. New York. 1986.

History of the Second World War, B. H. Liddell Hart. A Perigee/Putnam Book. New York. 1971.

Hitler: The Man and the Myth, Roger Manvell and Heinrich Fraenkel. Grafton Books/Collins Publishing Group. London, Glascow, Toronto. 1986.

The Marshall Cavendish Illustrated Encyclopedia of World War II, Brigadier General James L. Collins. New York London. 1985.

The United States and World War II: Miliary and Diplomatic Documents, ed. A. Rusell Buchanan. Harper and Row Publishers, New York, San Francisco, London. 1972.

World War II — Time Life Books, Alexandria, Virginia. 1980.

World War II in Cartoon, ed. Mark Bryant. Gallery Books, W. H. Smith Publishers, New York. 1989.

Writers and Readers Beginners Books

African History for Beginners ....8.95 _____
Architecture for Beginners..7.95 _____
Black History for Beginners...7.95 _____
Black Women for Beginners...8.95 _____
The Brain for Beginners ....8.95 _____
Brecht for Beginners ....7.95 _____
Capitalism for Beginners ....6.95 _____
Computers for Beginners ....7.95 _____
Cuba for Beginners ....6.95 _____
Darwin for Beginners..6.95 _____
DNA for Beginners ....6.95 _____
Ecology for Beginners ....6.95 _____
Economists for Beginners ....4.95 _____
Einstein for Beginners ....6.95 _____
Elvis for Beginners ....6.95 _____
Erotica for Beginners..8.95 _____
Food for Beginners...7.95 _____
French Revolution for Beginners...7.95 _____
Freud for Beginners ....6.95 _____
Hemingway for Beginners ....8.95 _____
Ireland for Beginners..6.95 _____
Judaism for Beginners ....7.95 _____
Lenin for Beginners..6.95 _____
London for Beginners...6.95 _____
Malcolm X for Beginners ....8.95 _____
Mao for Beginners..6.95 _____
Marx for Beginners...6.95 _____
Marx for Beginners (Second Edition) ....8.95 _____
Marx's *Kapital* for Beginners ....6.95 _____
Media and Communications for Beginners ....8.95 _____
Medicine for Beginners ....4.95 _____
Nicaragua for Beginners ....7.95 _____
Nietzsche for Beginners ....7.95 _____
Nuclear Power for Beginners ....6.95 _____
Orwell for Beginners...4.95 _____
Pan-Africanism for Beginners ....8.95 _____
Peace for Beginners...6.95 _____
Philosophy for Beginners ....8.95 _____
Plato for Beginners ....7.95 _____
Psychiatry for Beginners ....6.95 _____
Rainforests for Beginners...8.95 _____
Reagan for Beginners ....4.95 _____
Reich for Beginners..6.95 _____
Sex for Beginners...7.95 _____
Socialism for Beginners ....6.95 _____
Trotsky for Beginners ....6.95 _____
U.S. Constitution for Beginners...7.95 _____
Virginia Woolf for Beginners...7.95 _____
World War II for Beginners..8.95 _____
Zen for Beginners...6.95 _____